IF I'D
KNOWN
THEN

IF I'D
KNOWN
THEN

· ✳ ·

Women in Their 20s
and 30s Write Letters to
Their Younger Selves

Edited by
Ellyn Spragins

Da Capo
∞
LIFE
LONG

Designed by Cynthia Young
Set in 11 point Adobe Caslon

Cataloging-in-Publication data for this
book is available from the Library of Congress.

ISBN-13: 978-0-7382-1120-6

Published by Da Capo Press
A Member of the Perseus Books Group
www.dacapopress.com

Da Capo Press books are available at special discounts for
bulk purchases in the U.S. by corporations, institutions, and
other organizations. For more information, please contact the
Special Markets Department at the Perseus Books Group,
2300 Chestnut Street, Suite 200, Philadelphia, PA 19103,
or call (800) 255-1514, or e-mail
special.markets@perseusbooks.com.

10 9 8 7 6 5 4 3 2 1

For my father, Pete Spragins,
whose glad heart colors my life.

Contents

INTRODUCTION

If this is the first time you've held a book from the *What I Know Now*™ series in your hand, I'd like you to think of it as a gift—from me, from the generous young women whose letters are featured here, and from my mother, Joyce Spragins, who inspired the concept contained in these books. Unlike many books that contain advice, rules, and mandates about how to live your life, this book will not tell you to do anything. That's because each of the letters here is written by an accomplished young woman to *herself* at a younger age, with guidance, encouragement, or a warning she wished she'd been given at that time in her life. *If I'd Known Then: Women in Their 20s and 30s Write Letters to Their Younger Selves* captures those moments of twenty-twenty hindsight we all experience about our own lives.

Who knows better than Danica McKellar—the actress who played Winnie on *The Wonder Years*—what she needed to hear when she spent hours finding fault with herself in the mirror and days wondering why the object of her crush didn't call?

Who knows better than Olympic gymnast Amanda Borden what advice would have helped her thrive at the pressure-packed, elite level of competition when she was fifteen?

Learning the words of advice that a woman would give to herself, if she could somehow post a letter back in time, offers an intimate glimpse of who she was on the inside and what she struggled with at a particular juncture of her life. We can read these letters simply to understand more about fascinating women, such as Spanx founder Sara Blakely or Misty Copeland, the first African American ballerina to become a soloist in the American Ballet Theatre. Or we can discover that the hard-earned wisdom that would have helped Sara through the experience of her best friend's death or aided Misty through what she thought was a career-threatening moment actually applies to our own life.

Or we may understand, with a jolt of recognition, that we're not the only one who has felt this way. That realization can be a surprisingly powerful salve that brings comfort at the same time that it binds us to one another.

For this book I chose to focus on young women writing to themselves during their teenage and college years for a couple of reasons. After *What I Know Now: Letters to My Younger Self* ™ was published in 2006, I found myself inscribing great numbers of books destined to be given as gifts and graduation presents to teenagers and college-age women. I later received glowing reports from many of these young women. My own daughter, Keenan, who was then eighteen, stayed up all night reading the book with one of her best friends. (Yes, I know she's my daughter. But her list of favorite late-night activities does not usually include reading.) These young women seemed *hungry* for the insights and true experiences of other women.

Also, when I invited readers, Web site visitors, and audiences to write their own letters to their younger self (and send them to me at www.letterstomyyoungerself.com), I noticed that almost every letter was aimed at ages twelve to twenty-two. Those years bracket such enormous physical and emotional change that it's no surprise they are packed with difficult moments and turbulent periods. It's a measure of the intensity of those ages that women, who could pick any time in their life to send a message to, thought they needed the most help as a thirteen-year-old or sixteen-year-old or twenty-year-old.

What kind of life wisdom does a twenty-four-year-old have, really? Not much, I thought at first. But when I reflected upon the distance traveled between ages thirteen and sixteen, just three short years, or between junior year in high school and junior year in college, I began to change my mind. Women in their twenties and thirties may not have acquired life wisdom in every arena, but they have enough distance to know intimately what would have helped smooth their way through the thickets of cliques, bad boyfriends, bullies, unwise friendships, and family traumas that snagged them in middle shcool, high school, and college. That is the age group represented here, except for a couple of letter writers who left their thirties recently and a couple who are just edging out of their teens. These women were extremely opinionated about their messages.

Picked on because of her mixed racial background and her refusal to join a crowd, actress Jessica Alba dived into acting at thirteen because it meant she could get out of the hateful atmosphere at school. "Because I felt so alone when I was a kid, I really love young women. I think they are incredibly underestimated," she told me.

Confidence on the soccer field was never a problem for two-time World Cup champion, two-time Olympic gold medalist, and Olympic silver medalist Julie Foudy. But entering high school with "concave boobs" and short hair shriveled her self-assurance. "Looks are temporary. Strengths are not," she counsels her younger self.

The enormity of what some young women had to deal with and overcome as teenagers was humbling. Jewelry designer

Mindy Lam was considered an unlucky child by her Chinese father and was treated poorly compared to her sister and brother. Artist Tara McPherson essentially raised herself from age twelve because her alcoholic mother, with whom she lived, was absent or not functioning, and her father, whose house was nearby, often traveled the world for his work.

One theme in these letters surprised me, and one did not. Almost no one in the book truly felt they "fit in" or were "normal" during these years, even ostensibly successful cheerleaders, class presidents, and beauties. The absolute uniformity of every girl feeling different would be funny if the details weren't often so heartbreaking.

The unsurprising theme is how many girls wished to be skinny. I got the feeling that girls would have considered themselves pretty much untouchable if they could only be skinny. I don't blame the fashion industry or the media. I think skinniness is simply the handiest, just-possibly-attainable shield against slings and arrows and their own insecurities. It's more a measure of how desperately girls want some protective armor, or a magic power, than a rejection of their own bodies.

My desire to find out what I did not know, hard-won nuggets of wisdom, sparked *What I Know Now: Letters to My Younger Self™*. Yet I gained so much more than that. I discovered that these letters touch a deep place inside both letter writers and readers. The process of writing a letter to your younger self can bring closure. Sharing a letter can bring a wonderful connection that bridges differences among women.

I found that book clubs, women's groups, and reunion classes were reading the book and sharing their own letters to their younger selves. I began conducting women's leadership seminars for companies, using the concept of letter writing. Inspired by the idea which his wife, Kimberly

Williams-Paisley, told him about, country music star Brad Paisley wrote a sweet, wry song called "Letter To Me," aimed at his seventeen-year-old self. The music video was filmed at his old high school and some of the real-life people he mentions in the song have roles in the video.

All of this is to say that I now know enough not to know what will unfold after the publication of *If I'd Known Then*. But I do know it has been a privilege to meet and talk to the young women whose letters you are about to read. My wish is that they realize how much their words resonate with—and help—readers. And for readers, well, I hope for so much: less loneliness, more comfort, an escape from *your* little demon, whatever it may be. Most of all, I hope you see that *you are not the only one* and that *it won't be like this forever*. As Atoosa Rubenstein, founder of *CosmoGIRL!* and Alpha Kitty, says in her letter to her younger self, "You will find yourself in the future as you imagine yourself."

ACKNOWLEDGMENTS

I'm very grateful to the fascinating women in this book for participating and for opening up about a vulnerable time in their lives. You are the best. I would also like to express gratitude to the many indispensable assistants, publicists, relatives, and partners who facilitated the interviews, faxes, emails, and meetings, including Rebecca Kim, Candace Craig, Tamara Klosz Bonar, Meredith Howard, Becky Baumgartner, Maggie Adams, Galina Cohen, Roy Hofstetter, Meredith Howard, Janet Billig Rich, Kate Head, Shola Aleje, and Brad Cafarelli

My thanks also to my agent, Debra Goldstein, of The Creative Culture, and my editors from Da Capo Press, Wendy Holt and Marnie Cochran (now at Ballantine Books), whose confidence in the *What I Know Now* series has been so encouraging. Kate Burke, I appreciate your full-bore-ahead efforts on my behalf.

I was able to reach out to many of the letter writers with Erica Tannenbaum's essential, cheerful help and the critical support of her boss, Joanna Jordan, of Central Talent Booking. Alissa Molinelli also stepped in at the perfect time with a can-do attitude.

In addition, many friends and friends of friends offered to introduce me to some of the accomplished women who decided to participate in the book. I've come to depend on this serendipity, but it never fails to amaze me. I thank Laura Nolan,

Claire Mysko, Diana McNab, Kate Wood, Allison Kopicki, Judith Hamerman, Gerry Laybourne, Whitney LaRoche, Robin Carey, Amy Oringel, Theresa Patton, Claudia Harris, Connie Wilder, Betsy Battle, Lisa Cregan, and Eve Dryer.

My wise counselors and cheerleaders in life did not fail me with this project. I'm fortunate to have as friends Dottie Serdenis, Ouidad Wise, Cathryn Mitchell (aka Cathy Warrior Princess), John and Nancy Sivright, Diane DiResta, Jane Hubbard Jennings, Katie Bliss, Chris Miles, Janet Bamford, Lori Bongiorno, Kim Bonnell, Elizabeth Cahill, Kary Clancy, Meg Sieck, Debbie Lane, and the March 13th Book Club. I have also been lucky to make friends with many of the talented women who have invited me to speak and conduct seminars, including Susan Toroella, Melinda Wolfe, Anne Erni, Hope Greenfield, and Sara Daly.

I value the continuing support of Joyce Roche and Alex Kopelman from Girls Inc. and the high-voltage boost from Fearon Perry at YOU by Crocs, and Julie Fairweather at In Full Force.

To my family, near and far, thank you for the encouragement, coffee, and backrubs.

Jessica Alba

Actress

"Adults are not always right."

$\mathcal{J}$ESSICA ALBA may have a body that is foremost on the minds of adolescent boys and men who peruse *E!*'s Sexiest Celebrity Bodies list or *Maxim* magazine's Hot 100 roll. But girls—and what's on their minds—are whom the young actress actually cares about. "Because I felt so alone when I was a kid, I really love young women. I think they are incredibly underestimated," she says.

Her outsider status started with her mixed heritage. Her dad, who was in the U.S. Air Force, is Mexican, and her mom is white. When she was growing up in Mississippi, Texas, and California, Jessica said that people often thought her mother was her babysitter. "When you're not racially defined, they don't accept you in either culture," she explains.

But Jessica was also rejected by kids her own age, she thinks, because she was unwilling to follow the crowd. Neither smoking at lunch nor being a teacher's pet really interested her. Occasionally when kids picked on Jessica, her father would go to school in an effort to intimidate the bullies. But it didn't help. "I cried a lot. I didn't smile very often," she says of those years in sixth and seventh grade.

Two apparently contradictory paths helped her escape. From age thirteen to sixteen she became a born-again Christian. It gave her a sense of belonging and was her own way of rebelling against parents who were very cool and very liberal. "Some people need extreme forms of guidance to deal with life. It kept me out of trouble. Instead of going to parties and messing around, I was trying to bring people to the light," she says, looking back.

The other outlet was acting. Its biggest appeal, initially, was that it released Jessica from the daily misery of school. She spoke three lines in her first part, a role in a 1994 movie, *Camp Nowhere*, a gig that was supposed to last for only two weeks. Instead she worked for two months after an actress in the project dropped out. When she got her Screen Actors Guild card, it was the first time she felt accepted. It's also when she realized there might be an alternate route for her.

Her dad made her go back to school, but Jessica continued to audition for more jobs so she could stay out of the torture chamber. Before long, she was making enough money to hire a California-certified tutor. "I worked my ass off. I think that was the beginning of me taking my life into my own hands," she says.

Some of Jessica's best-known roles have been in the television series *Dark Angel* and *Flipper*, as well as in films such as *Sin City*, *Fantastic Four*, *Into the Blue*, and *Good Luck Chuck*. Although she is only twenty-six, she has already spent thirteen years building her career and advocates an early start for any girl. "If I could say anything to teenage girls it would be, 'You're not alone. You're not crazy. There is nothing holding you back,'" she says with conviction. "I wasn't given anything on a silver platter and now I get to reach out to young women who feel excluded."

In this letter, she writes to herself at the beginning of sixth grade, after two self-righteous PTA moms and the principal of her school called her to the nurse's office to accuse her of being a slut.

*

Dear Jessica,

Your head feels like it is going to burst. You tried not to cry when you walked out of the nurse's office and down the hall. The accusation still ricochets in your head.

They think I'm a slut??? I've never even had a boyfriend!!!

This is only the latest injustice. Kids pull your backpack off as you walk down the hall. They've kicked dirt in your food outside during lunch. And, as you see now, adults are no better.

They're all ignorant. The kids think something is wrong with you because you're developing early. The teachers don't encourage their students to think or question anything. They want textbook answers. And parents, especially the rich parents of white, soccer-playing kids, are the worst. They constantly criticize you and tear you apart.

All of this makes you think maybe you're crazy. You're so different, so impatient and so resentful of authority. Maybe that's wrong.

But you're not crazy, Jessica. Adults are not always right. Whatever you do, do not spend one second worrying about what kids your own age think. They are worthless right now.

One more thing. Boys are awful. They are made of nothing but hormones until they're about twenty or twenty-one. So, you just can't take relationships too seriously until you're older. You're going to change; what you want in life is going to change, and your taste is going to become more sophisticated. It's fun to have a crush, but don't think it's forever. You have the rest of your life to do that.

And use birth control and condoms, please.

Keep questioning and challenging,
Jessica

. ✳ .

Magali Amadei

Actress

*"Perfection as you imagine it
can never be attained."*

cMAGALI AMADEI'S secret started at about thirteen
or fourteen. Long before she became a top model whose face
and body regularly graced the covers of *Vogue, Glamour, Cos-
mopolitan,* and *Marie Claire,* she and a friend learned how to
make themselves throw up. Why? At first it was an occasional
experiment triggered by her setting. She grew up in Nice in
the south of France where "you're half naked year round," she
says. "I was very aware of how a body should look, and my
standard was a ballerina's body." Her perfectionist leanings
were intensified by her evolving sexual awareness and pubes-
cent hypersensitivity to a stray comment about her body looking "fat."

Before long, though, purging gave Magali a feeling of control. "You belittle yourself. You say to yourself, 'You're a loser.
You're nothing.' You feel so insignificant," she remembers.

As unhealthy as it was, a couple of factors made it easy—
almost natural, in fact—for her to keep her bulimia secret. Her
family's tradition was not to speak about uncomfortable topics.
Also, a sentence from *Candide*—one of Voltaire's novels—

echoed in her memory, but over time she misinterpreted and modified it. The original quote, roughly translated, is "Let us cultivate our garden." In her head she always thought the quote referred to a private garden that no one knew about. By her early teens she believed the quote, which she had imprinted clearly in her mind, meant that everyone had secrets that they put in their private garden.

So she threw up regularly, told no one, and at age seventeen was discovered by a modeling agent who saw her dancing a ballet. Magali persuaded her parents to let her try modeling for two weeks after graduating from high school. She arrived in the United States, started working after two days, and within two months had magazine covers, bank accounts, and an apartment.

"It's ironic because it's the worst place for someone suffering with poor body image. Being on a magazine cover reassured me that I was a loser who was trumping everyone. In addition to already being someone with a secret, I became lonelier and lonelier because I was away from my support system," she says.

Now, Magali speaks regularly about eating disorders at universities, high schools, and conferences, in partnership with Claire Mysko, a former director of the American Anorexia Bulimia Association who is now a freelance writer and Web consultant. Their goal is to educate girls about the dangers of comparing themselves to unattainable images. Magali continues to model occasionally and began acting in 2000. She has appeared in the film *Taxi*, starring Queen Latifah, the HBO comedy series *The Mind of a Married Man*, and in David Duchovny's *House of D*. In recent months she began working on a book, tentatively titled *Beauty-Baby Balance: A Guide for Any Woman Who Has Considered Opting Out of Mommyhood to Avoid Weighing In*.

Along with these career developments and her role as mother of two-year-old Chloe, Magali has worked very hard on a far more private restorative task: reaching back and taking care of the young girl-child who she had been. "Even now, when I think about it, I cannot believe how much I abandoned myself all those years. I feel like I left my own little girl-self in a corner. I turned my back to her and started walking on the road to being an adult," says Magali. Now thirty-four, Magali is writing to herself just before she turned fourteen.

Dear Mag,

The title of this letter is *It's Not Worth the Pain.*

You've started thinking that if you were a perfect girl, all your torment would go away, that you wouldn't have to hide from anyone—including yourself and your own feelings. That word "perfection" will haunt you more than you can expect. I wish you could know that perfection, as you imagine it, can never be attained; that kind of perfection doesn't exist.

You will begin to understand this when you sit for hours having your makeup and hair done. You will be photographed for dozens of major fashion magazines, and every single picture will be retouched. You are not those glossy images because the real you is, well, *real.* Learn to accept yourself for who you are. Stop judging and comparing yourself to others. You make mistakes, and so does everybody else. There is no shame in not having all the answers. Being wrong is not the end of the world. There is no need to be that hard on yourself. It is a waste of time.

You will forget how to say "I love you" to your own reflection, and it will take you years to be able to say it again.

Please, throw away your scale! It will become your worst enemy. Don't start dieting. You'll be fooled by a false sense of power, and it will trigger something that will end up controlling you. Trust me, diets don't work. You are not as fat as you imagine. Every time you throw up, it is a sign you are trying to control yourself and numb your feelings.

Instead, I want you to talk about everything. As hard as it might be, I want you to cry, scream, and laugh. Don't try to erase emotions or push them down. When you do share what's inside of you, I promise you will discover that you are not alone.

I want you to know that your hormones are much stronger than you think, and they are responsible for a lot of what you are feeling. Of course what you are feeling is still real, but it is terribly exaggerated by natural chemical changes in your body.

More than anything else, though, I want to tell you now, before it is too late, that it's not worth the shame or the pain to have secrets. You know the big secret I'm talking about. Secrets are a difficult weight to bear. No one should have any secret that she couldn't tell to at least one other person.

For seven years you will tell no one your secret. It will not only be too heavy to carry, but it will make you lonelier and lonelier. And it will become way too dangerous.

You will eventually vomit as many as seven times a day. Stomach acid will eat away the enamel of your teeth, eventually causing you to get seven caps, a bridge, two implants, and eleven root canals. You will begin taking laxatives and have a complete collapse.

Right now you are not so far away from that happy, attentive little girl you used to be. Don't leave her behind or you will end up missing yourself. Take care of her, and she will probably take care of you, too.

Seeing the sun on you,
Magali

. ✳ .

NATASHA BEDINGFIELD

Singer/Songwriter

"Some parts of life have to be messy
before they can become beautiful."

*W*HEN I spoke to Natasha Bedingfield, she had just
returned from seven or eight months in the United States, an
unexpectedly long trip due to the success of her debut album,
Unwritten. The title song became one of the most successful
singles of 2006, selling more than one million digital down-
loads and being nominated in the category of Best Female Pop
Performance at the 49th Grammy Awards.

After eighteen months away from England, Natasha was
happily settling into her new home: a three-bedroom house in
the southwest part of London. In between having the house
painted and having an old ceiling taken down, she was empty-
ing moving boxes and rediscovering bits of her past. "I'm finding cards from old boyfriends and the suit I wore for my first
job, doing reception work, after I quit university," she said,
laughing at the hominess of such domestic treasures.

We don't usually think of rock stars, particularly glossy ones
with Natasha's long, blonde hair, perfect teeth, and lavishly
mascaraed, sexy eyes, as having struggled. But as a young teen

Natasha felt confined by circumstances and her responsibilities. Her parents were from New Zealand, which made her always feel like a bit of an outsider. Rather than being direct, she was keenly aware that the British culture prized subtlety and overzealous politeness.

As the oldest girl in a family of four kids, Natasha was also the responsible one who looked after the other kids and kept the peace among them. (Her older brother Daniel is also a singer-songwriter.) "Everyone said I was mature. I liked that, but it also kind of kept me from being free to be a kid. Looking back, I was so afraid of making a mistake. I wanted to keep everyone happy," she said.

Music and art helped her learn how to express herself and become more experimental. She remembers taking an art course when she was fourteen and how hard she tried to paint her subject perfectly in every detail. The teacher urged her to paint the whole picture in broad strokes instead. "She said, 'Do the overall picture—do whatever you can see now.' It was this freeing moment," recalls Natasha.

Although she still has to fight her inclination to be the constant peacemaker, she marvels at the freedom her musical career offers. "I feel like it's amazing that I do write songs and that they are often quite daring. They give me permission to be a bit crazy."

Natasha released *N.B.*, her highly regarded second album, in 2007 and also performed for five weeks with Justin Timberlake's FutureSexLoveShow summer tour. Now twenty-six, Natasha is writing to herself at thirteen.

＊

Dear Natasha,

You're the person who doesn't cause any fuss. You don't make extra work for anyone. You don't complain or make demands. You put the greater good ahead of your own desires.

All of that is what turned you into "the responsible one" in your family, and you know how important and helpful that is to your parents. Still, Natasha, you sometimes take it too far. You care more about people who don't like you than the ones who do. You have trouble saying "No" when people ask too much of you because you're afraid of losing their good opinion.

Sometimes you are your own worst enemy. Don't be so serious. Don't despise where you're at. Instead, try enjoying it. Realize that you can't make *everyone* like you—there's always someone who won't. You will find this hard to believe, but in your case making a fuss and being disliked by someone will reflect progress. They'll be signs that you are finally giving voice to your true self.

You won't be able to go in that direction until you understand that some parts of life have to be messy before they can become beautiful. Not long from now you will try to write songs in your diary and find yourself despising them for being so babyish. A singer friend will suggest a new approach: Work at writing songs every day without critiquing them. That's how the muscles develop. That's how the songs will get better.

Years from now you will write a song for your younger brother about embracing life fully, but the message will be just as important for you as for him. "Release your inhibitions / Feel the rain on your skin / No one else can feel it for you / Only you can let it in."

Love,
Your not-so-perfect future self

· ✳ ·

SARA BLAKELY

Founder of Spanx

"If you weren't afraid, would you do it?"

*Y*OU'D think the founder of Spanx, the stretchy body shapers that are the solution to panty lines, muffin-tops, and jiggly spots, would look like someone who actually needs figure enhancement. But no. Sara Blakely at thirty-six looks like the cheerleader she once was: slender and well-proportioned. Her long, blonde-streaked hair bounces a little as she moves quickly through her Atlanta office, wearing jeans with heels. She has a camera-ready smile and the kind of determination you don't expect to find in a pretty girl.

In 1998 at age twenty-seven, Sara cut the feet out of her control-top pantyhose to solve the problem of what to wear under her new white pants. She worked on her idea for two years in her apartment at night, while selling office equipment during the day. Her concept—comfortable body slimmers coupled with light-hearted packaging and names—was a gust of fresh air in the tired hosiery industry. "Let's not suck it up," Spanx seems to say to us—"let's get some help, sister!" And here it is: Bra-llelujah!, Higher Power Panties, Slim Cognito, and Hide & Sleek to the rescue. In 2006, Sara made another huge leap toward streamlining America when she launched ASSETS by Sara Blakely, a brand found at Target stores.

The reception area in Spanx's office may be the only one in corporate America that looks like a cross between a bordello and a nightclub. The room practically glows with the company's signature red on the walls. A round, fuchsia velvet seat is rimmed with fringe. Ruffled organza curtains frame the doorways, and a video monitor replays Spanx's debut on *The Oprah Winfrey Show* in 2000. While I was visiting, a production crew for *American Inventor*, an ABC reality show, arrived, toting lights and cameras. Sara was one of four judges for the show's second season, which aired in 2007.

It all sounds very glamorous and a little effortless. But some of Sara's success, odd as it sounds, is connected to tragedy. Between the ages of sixteen and twenty-two, she mourned the deaths of eight friends (two of whom had been prom dates) who each passed away from separate, devastating accidents. At the age of thirty-one, tragedy struck again when her best friend and roommate in Atlanta was hit by a car and killed while riding a horse. "I definitely live my life with a sense of urgency," she told me, while eating lunch at her desk. "I know that has a lot to do with all the death I've experienced because deep down I think 'I have this opportunity to do something that they don't have.'"

The death of her friend Susie happened five feet in front of Sara in Clearwater, Florida, where they grew up. It was the summer between sophomore and junior year for Sara. Susie was a year older. The two were riding bikes back to the beach over a narrow bridge after indulging in a Taco Bell meal. Susie's handlebar hit a generator that had been left on the sidewalk by a construction crew, causing her to lose her balance momentarily. To catch herself she leaned out into the road right in front of a car.

With tremendous sadness, Sara recounts, "A car ran over her, the front tires and the back tires. I just dropped my bike and ran up to her. She was curled up in a ball by the side of the road." Sara pauses a moment as she recalls the blood coming from Susie's mouth, nose, and ears. "I must have been in shock because the first thing I said to her was, 'Susie, Susie, I have to get you out of the road because I don't want you to get hit by a car,'" she remembers. The severity of the accident did not begin to sink in until a woman from seemingly nowhere warned her not to touch Susie because her back might be injured. "What do you mean her back might be injured?" Sara remembers asking.

Overnight the bubbly, high-energy girl who had been at the center of everything—both cheerleader and debate team member, friend to popular kids, nerds, and middle grounders— became very introspective. For the first time in her life, she felt isolated. This letter is written to herself after Susie's death, during the period of time when Sara would ride her bike fifteen minutes from her house to the beach, where she spent evening after evening by herself watching the sun set, trying to come to her own understanding of the meaning of life.

Dear Sara,

It's amazing to have friends who you can be silly with in one moment and in the next seriously discuss your wildest dreams and greatest fears. I know Susie was a friend like that for you, especially during summers when you had ample time to get lost on your bikes in the hot Florida sun. You are blessed to have had a friend like that, and by keeping your heart open, you will continue to have such relationships for the rest of your life.

It may be difficult to see right now, but you have just been given an enormous life lesson at a shockingly young age. You just realized how precious and fleeting life is. You were faced with your own mortality, a subject most people choose to avoid and don't have to face until much later in life. This can devastate you or motivate you—it's your choice. Always look for the hidden blessings, even in your darkest moments; I promise they are there. You cannot control many things that will happen to you, but you can control how you see them.

Choose to see them in a way that lifts you up, not brings you down.

When well-meaning people say, "Sara, I'm so sorry you had to go through this," you respond, "You know what? I'm actually very lucky because I was the one chosen to spend the last couple of minutes of Susie's life with her."

The truths you are discovering here may be the most fundamental drivers of your future. You are right—there are no guarantees about life continuing. Susie's death is not the only one that will imprint that lesson on you. Eventually, you will develop a mantra that sums up the sense of urgency you feel about seizing life: *I don't want to just get through something. I want to get through it and soar.*

Train yourself to go to the positive. Always. You gravitate toward this approach already, but it's going to become imperative. Your father will give you a ten-tape series by Wayne Dyer called *How to Be a No-Limit Person* when he and Mom decide to divorce.

I can't tell you what a blessing those tapes will be in your life. You will listen to them over and over. You will learn to live your life and make decisions despite what other people think. It's a freedom that allows you to take more risks and achieve more success. You will learn to trust your gut and inner voice as your guide and life compass.

You will learn these lessons so well that they will become ingrained—and you'll be astonished at what you'll be able to accomplish. You'll start a successful company and star in a reality television show with Richard Branson (chairman of The Virgin Group). He will help you start The Sara Blakely Foundation which will allow you to help other women realize their dreams.

Here is one of the tricks that will help you move forward quickly. When weighing opportunities, you'll pose a question to yourself: "If you weren't afraid, would you do it?" If the answer is "Yes," you'll force yourself to do it. You won't ever want fear to get in the way of taking action. You'll reason with yourself: *If I'm alive, am I going to let something as stupid and irrational as fear get in the way of going for this—of getting on a stage, starting a company, or giving a speech?* They will all terrify you, but do them anyway. You will be amazed at how your life will flourish.

Be good to yourself, and be good to your life, even when it presents you with something as alarming and tragic as the loss of a beautiful, vibrant friend. Don't shut yourself off from your life and the people in it. Stay true to your nature. You were given a gregarious, curious, fun-loving, thoughtful self. Use it to the best of your abilities.

Stay vulnerable. Take risks. Live unafraid of failures because failures are evidence that you tried and that is a wonderful thing. Stay motivated by remembering those who no longer have the opportunities you have. Draw strength and courage from their spirit.

I'm proud of you—and so is Susie.
Sara

. ✻ .

AMANDA BORDEN

Olympic Gymnast

*"To achieve your potential, you'll have to
rediscover the joy."*

SMALL, blonde, and happy, Amanda Borden is someone
who people love to be around. You may know her as captain of
the first U.S. gymnastics team to win an Olympic gold medal
at the 1996 games in Atlanta. But think of this: She was also
popular enough to be voted the 1994 Homecoming Queen at
Finneytown High School. Amanda's affability is the reason
she became captain of the Magnificent Seven, as they were
called. When the seven team members cast their votes,
Amanda voted for Shannon Miller, but everyone else voted for
Amanda.

"I was not the best athlete on the team—not close to it," she
says, from Tempe, Arizona, where Amanda and her husband,
Brad Cochran, run Gold Medal Gym. "But I felt like I could
give them something else." That something else was a certain
freedom of spirit that she experienced during competition,
which she was able to convey to her teammates.

You could have seen that expansive attitude during much
of her childhood. Born and raised in Cincinnati, Amanda
loved gymnastics so much at age seven that when she began
classes, she begged her mother for more than the once-a-week

session. But by the time she was fifteen and switched to the highly demanding, elite level of competition, she began to crack under the pressure. Here is her letter to herself during that period.

*

Dear Pepsodent,

I'm using the nickname that the media has given you because it has a message for you: The joy you used to have in gymnastics can still be there. Remember that feeling? Fun. It was always present during all the years you practiced and competed. Now that you're in elite, though, there is so much pressure you are overwhelmed. It's like you've moved from playing in the sandbox to trudging through quicksand. It almost doesn't feel like the same sport.

Focusing on goals instead of fun is making you falter under pressure. You want to quit. You feel like maybe the only way to become a world champion or an Olympic athlete is to be like so many of the girls you compete against—kids who thrive under pressure.

But even though no one talks about it, there is more than one way to get to the Olympics. *You* are different from the pressure-junkies. For you to achieve your potential, you'll have to rediscover the joy you've always had. There will be someone who will help you with this. She will teach you something you'll be able to use your whole life. Take one thing at a time.

Don't think about how you always fall off the balance beam in competition—or always wobble. She'll teach you a trick, which is to recite a few words for each move in your routine when you're practicing. Then, when you're in competition, the words will prompt a comfortable focus on each part.

Easy run. Feet in front. Over the top. Come on. You get it.

Simple—but this technique will put that Pepsodent smile back on your face because it will allow the joy to surface again.

By the time you are seventeen you will be able to stay on that balance beam in competition. One day, during the Olympics, you'll be secure enough to comfort a crying teammate by telling her, "We've practiced so hard and done everything we can. Now it's in God's hands, and what we need to do is go out there and enjoy ourselves."

All your life people will know you for the gold medals you and your team won, but you will feel just as much pride in your role there. You'll carry the unique message about using joy to be successful into the coaching of young gymnasts. And that's an even bigger legacy.

Your friend,
Amanda

. ✳ .

EMILY BRYDON

Olympic Skier

*"Bury that temptation to conform to society
as soon as possible."*

$\mathcal{E}$MILY BRYDON, a Canadian Olympic skier, grew up in a beautiful cocoon of a childhood. Her mother and father built their log home themselves on ten acres in Fernie, a ski resort in British Columbia. She was an only child who spent a lot of time with her parents and their friends. Money was short. The family didn't have a television, and her mother made all of Emily's clothing until she was in eighth grade. Enveloped in her parents' self-sufficiency, however, Emily didn't notice a lack.

"Mine was always the birthday party to come to because my mother made them so fun, with scavenger hunts, treasure hunts, games, and great goodie bags. She's a really good baker, and I always had the baking to give to people," recalls Emily.

She spent a lot of time playing outside, often with her father. He passed on his love of skiing and sports to Emily. By the time she was in high school, she was well on her way to her ultimate height of six feet and had become a serious competitive skier, training and competing all over the world. She was in the popular group at school, but she felt her status there was shaky—always needing to be shored up.

On a powder-coated mountain, however, she felt perfectly at ease. "It feels like total freedom. It allows me to express myself. I'm such a driven person, it's an avenue for me to use that drive," she says.

Emily's talents were amply displayed in 2005 at the Pontiac GMC Canadian Alpine Championships where she was a gold medalist in the Downhill, Super-G, Slalom, and Combined disciplines. The last time those awards had been won by a single competitor was almost forty years earlier. More recently, she was ranked ninth in the Super-G and also ninth in Combined in the world.

Jetting from one beautiful mountain to another all over the world, in order to do exactly what she wants, makes her feel privileged—and a bit guilty at times. So in 2006 she established the Emily Brydon Youth Foundation, which is designed to offer financial support to kids who want to pursue interests in arts or athletics or who want to further their education.

Though she was intensely dedicated to her career at a young age, there was a period when she doubted her direction and questioned whether she should continue. Then, her father died of cancer in 1998 when she was eighteen years old. It was a turning point on many levels. One outcome was that she might have to stop skiing without the financial support her father had provided. A local family who was friendly with Emily's family and whose kids participated in ski racing stepped in, offering their support. That's when Emily decided to truly do what was right for her and commit herself to the sport—in part as a way of honoring her father. Here Emily, twenty-seven, writes to her younger self between the ages of seventeen and nineteen, when she questioned her skiing career.

*

Dear Emily,

 This back-and-forth on your ski-racing career is confusing you. Clearly you're dedicated and a hard worker, but you're wondering if it's really right for you.

 It is.

 You have no way of recognizing this now, so let me spell it out. You doubt yourself because you're encountering tremendous resistance from your environment. You're trying to speed down a mountain with a giant parachute ballooning out behind you.

 Look at your social life. You're in the popular group because you have such an exotic life, zipping off to other states and different countries for the winter and then popping back. But you miss so much of what your friends experience that you're constantly playing catch up. Getting back into the social system is really stressful.

 Then there are the teachers, who are making your life miserable. They seem to resent your absences, even though you work harder than other kids and you're an A student. One of your teachers told you dismissively that he doesn't have time for you in class now. Teachers seem willing to accommodate the schedules of ambitious male hockey players—but an ambitious female athlete goes against the norm. Society is so strict about what teenagers should do and how to become the perfect career woman.

You and your parents will have to fight the school system for months to allow you to move to Whistler and do your schoolwork there. For you, the fight will be to prove to the school that women in sports are legitimate and should be respected and supported. Your frustration over the administration's inability to see outside the box will make you feel so angry.

These headwinds get you down. You spend a lot of time justifying your devotion to your sport. But the worst part of all this, Emily, is the flak you are creating for yourself. You are a people-pleaser. You know what you believe in, but you're afraid to voice it because you don't fully trust yourself, and you want to fit in.

Bury that temptation to conform to society, as soon as possible!

Do you know what that means? *Trust yourself.* When you face big decisions in life, it's perfectly fine to ask others what they think. But when it comes down to actually doing it, you are way better off following your gut.

What if your gut is silent? Wait. Wait until you hear your intuition. It's almost always correct.

xxoo
Emily

. ✳ .

Rebecca Budig

Actress

"Fortune favors the bold."

Raised in Fort Mitchell, Kentucky, Rebecca Budig attended the School for Creative and Performing Arts in Cincinnati, Ohio, before arriving at Miami University of Ohio. A future star of two soaps, *Guiding Light* and *All My Children*, Rebecca wandered through her first year and part of the second, feeling vaguely out of place at the idyllic, mostly white college. "The student body was very racially diverse at my high school; so for me, Miami was a culture shock," she remembers.

That wasn't the only feature of college life that left her unsettled. She had a boyfriend who was part of a fraternity, so she found herself going to Greek parties, even though she was never a sorority girl. She just didn't seem to fit in with her college life.

None of this was terribly painful, but it became all the more confusing when her manager suggested that she go to Los Angeles during pilot season. It meant leaving college during the spring semester of her sophomore year—and it meant leaving her boyfriend. Her parents supported her choice, but they would not make the decision for her. She felt it was a now-or-never moment, time to make a big leap. The prospect of change was exciting—but part of her was fearful about leaving her boyfriend and being so far away from home and family. Part of her was nervous about being judged for leaving college.

Now married to TV host Bob Guiney, Rebecca had finished a role in Lifetime's *A Perfect Child*, completed a starring guest role on *CSI*, and recently become the happy owner of a puppy in the months before we spoke. For the student who once planned to be a vet, it's heaven. Here Rebecca, thirty-four, writes to herself as a college sophomore trying to make up her mind.

Dear Becky,

Do it. Go! Don't allow fear to hold you back! Most people, you will find as you get older, make all of their choices and decisions based in fear. Don't be a victim to that!

With change comes growth—whether good or bad. So you leave your boyfriend? If it's truly meant to be, it will be. If you never challenge yourself, you'll never know what you're capable of . . . and how far you can go!

Think about what your chemistry teacher said: "You could do very well in your zoology major, but your heart's not really in it. Follow your passion. Why not go?"

And as your acting teacher once said to you, "Fortune favors the bold. Be bold. Because your fortune awaits you!"

Love,
Rebecca

• ✳ •

PHOTO: JEAN RENARD

SASHA COHEN
Olympic Skater

*"It's possible to make something hard
in your own mind."*

SEEING Olympic silver medalist Sasha Cohen in person—
that is, seeing how little there is of her—you'd never guess that
she and her mother, Galina, are ardent foodies. We met for
lunch in the formal dining room of The Modern, which is the
Museum of Modern Art's temple to creative food combina-
tions. The spare, delicate constructions on our square plates
seemed to complement the sculpture garden just outside the
window.

And the restaurant could not have attracted a more attentive customer. Sasha deconstructs her meals a fork-tine's worth
at a time, identifying ingredients and tossing off culinary
terms, such as *amuses-bouche* and *beurre manié*, like a veteran
kitchen jockey. She also loves to share, giving away most of the
parsley fritters, the intricate Napoleon, and almost everything
else set before her. That explains her slender stalk of a figure—
and speaks volumes about the iron will inside it. She may look
like a fresh-faced young thing, but make no mistake, Sasha
Cohen is unapologetically confident about what she wants in
life—and what she doesn't.

A conventional skating career ending at age twenty-five? Well, no. After winning the U.S. gold medal, the Olympic silver medal, and a bronze in the 2006 World Figure Skating Championships, she decided at twenty-one to buck expectations and take a break. "You work to achieve this shining moment, but you can work and work and still not have it. It was so intense. That's why I stopped competing. I couldn't do it for another four years," she says.

Acting? Yes. Sasha is sure it's for her. After small roles in *Las Vegas, CSI: NY, Project Runway,* and *Blades of Glory,* she got her first role playing someone other than Sasha Cohen in *Moondance Alexander,* which opened in the fall of 2007. Earlier that year, she completed a five-week theater fundamentals course at the Moscow Art Summer Academy on Harvard University's campus, where her Russian heritage (her mother is Ukrainian) excited her fellow students. In between hobnobbing with celebrities at Hollywood functions, taking acting lessons at home in Los Angeles, and appearing on behalf of numerous charities, such as the Figure Skating Club of Harlem, she tours with Champions on Ice and Smucker's Stars on Ice.

College? Not yet. "I used to think that I did not need the college experience to accomplish my goals," she explains. The experience at Harvard changed her mind, however, and she now looks forward eagerly to attending in the future.

In the meantime, she hasn't abandoned the business of making the whole world's heart stop by whirling multiple times in the air, hiking her splits up into Vs, and becoming a living filigree on ice. She hopes to skate in the 2010 Olympics. By taking time off from competitions, "I got back that love of skating. I still in my heart feel like I'm not done," she says.

Now twenty-three, Sasha writes to herself when she was seventeen, the year she first qualified for the Olympics and thought she could do absolutely everything. "I decided to make the Olympics, learn the quad and the triple triple, go to high school so I could go to prom—and go to skating events around the world," she remembers.

✳

Dear Sasha,

You've never had a problem with dreaming and aspiring and wanting. You reach for the moon. Are you practical? Logical? No—not you! You want everything that you can possibly dream of.

You never say, "I can't."

I'm not writing to tell you to change that. Far from it. But I do want to tell you something to watch out for: doubt. The only thing that you'll find that can hold you back is the doubt that comes from over-thinking and trying so hard to be flawless that no one could measure up.

Trust. That is what you should do rather than doubt.

Most people get in their own way. It's possible to make something hard in your own mind. When you're going to do something anyway, whether it's acting or skating, your life would be so much easier if you just did it with trust rather than thinking too much about it. Thinking and worrying are the nemesis of perfection.

You have to trust your body and go with it. Because you're an athlete you know how much trust has to do with being present—not thinking about yesterday's practice, or four years from now.

You have set some truly ambitious goals for yourself this year, so many that it will be easy to fret over them. Remember that you can't be your best unless you are here. The mind can do only one thing at a time. So give everything you have to *this* moment.

With confidence, always,
Sasha

· ✳ ·

MISTY COPELAND

Dancer, American Ballet Theatre

*"The path to your success is not as fixed and
inflexible as you think."*

MOST of us hope to discover within ourselves a talent so
sparkling and pronounced that it's obvious to everyone. That's
exactly what happened to Misty Copeland, the first African
American ballerina to become a soloist at the American Ballet
Theatre. She started dancing at thirteen—woefully late by ballet standards—and knew instantly that this was what she was
meant for. Everyone who saw her dance knew it, too.

"Starting dance was like starting living," she recalls in a
quiet voice, sitting in a small meeting room in ABT's quarters
on lower Broadway. "I have always been such a shy person, and
I don't think I ever had my own voice. I was good in school. I
was a good kid. But I never really had found anything that
I was particularly great at or really enjoyed doing."

On stage, the shy girl—the fourth of six children raised in
San Pedro, California—became a natural performer. Dancing
gave her a voice, she claims, and what that voice says is: "I'm
someone special and strong and I know what I want. I don't
think you get that impression just from talking to me."

When I met Misty, she was about to turn twenty-five and
had recently been promoted from the company's corps de

ballet to Soloist. This ascension took six hard years. Only five feet three inches (but with big feet, she assured me—size eight), she has cocoa-colored skin and an upturned nose that gives her face a mischievous quality, which is countered by her soft-spoken, slightly bashful manner.

While it's a relief, the promotion also ups the ante for Misty. Once she got to New York in 2000, she discovered for the first time that being a black ballerina is a big deal. It had never been an issue in California, but at ABT no African American had ever progressed beyond the corps. Being the first feels tremendously validating, but she was already sensing heightened expectations at her new level.

This challenge, however, doesn't begin to approach the crisis Misty experienced at fifteen, only two years after she started dancing. Because her mother could not transport her to the small ballet school she attended, at thirteen Misty had moved in with her teacher's family. Enthralled with newly discovered passion, she loved the total immersion. After two years, though, Misty's mother, who had become more financially settled, wanted her daughter to move back home. Misty says that her teacher urged her to pursue "emancipation," a legal procedure by which minors can declare themselves adults. It would mean she could choose whom she lived with and where she danced.

"At the time, I don't think I was completely aware of what emancipation meant. This was all my teacher's idea. She just thought my mother couldn't raise me the way a dancer and someone going places needed to be raised," says Misty.

Misty's mother moved her daughter back home. A court fight ensued, and Misty's emancipation request was withdrawn because she was too young to qualify. Her letter is to herself at fifteen when she had just moved back in with her mother and the court fight was raging.

*

Dear Misty,

I know what you're thinking: What does your mother know about dance and ballet? *Nothing!* It seems like what she wants is going to stand in the way of everything you have been working for.

All you know for sure is that you want to dance. That's all you were trying to do. Your heroine, Paloma Herrera at the ABT, joined the company when she was fifteen. Desire to get on with it, to become a professional, to become who you were meant to be, thunders in your heart. Fear that you won't, that now you can't possibly make it, races through your stomach.

School is horrible. Because of the court case, all your business is out there on the news and in the papers for everyone to see. Everyone at school knows.

Now you feel shut off from everyone. There is no one to talk to about any of this—and you don't want to, anyway. You cry by yourself every night.

You've created an equation in your mind that says you won't make it to the ABT if you can't stay with the teacher who practically invented your life in ballet. But one day you'll look back and realize that she did not care for you as a person as much as you thought. She cares for you as a dancer and wants to attach herself to your success.

Misty, have a little faith in Mom. Trusting her feels almost impossible for you now . . . but try. She truly wants nothing but the best for you. The truth is, you don't need that teacher. The path to your success is not as fixed and inflexible as you think.

So much that's good for your career will come out of this change. You'll make great leaps in your new ballet school. You'll meet Ashley Ellis, who will become an important friend in your development. Your strengths and weaknesses will complement hers, so you'll push each other to get better in all the right places. All of that will lead not only you, but Ashley, to ABT.

Misty, you will live out your dream just as amazingly as you are hoping to!

The other great result is that you will have a wonderful relationship with your mother. When all the kids have grown and left, you'll choose to vacation with her, and she won't be able to stop smiling at you.

You, a Soloist in the American Ballet Theatre.

· ✳ ·

HOPE EDELMAN

Author

"Take risks. Take them now."

*H*OPE EDELMAN'S mother died of breast cancer when Hope was seventeen. Her death fell upon Hope all at once, like a blow. But the greater injury played out gradually, the way a busted tempered glass window slowly snaps and pops as tiny cracks appear and multiply over the course of a few days, finally obscuring the view with a web of broken glass. The loss of her mother, she gradually understood, was not a discrete event. Grief sank its tentacles into her and lacerated her insides periodically, and sometimes, it seemed, arbitrarily.

One lasting consequence of Hope's experience is a book whose title is proffered by friends and acquaintances in the same way a doctor might ask about a patient's home remedies. "Have you read *Motherless Daughters* by Hope Edelman?" That was the question put to me so often on a book tour that I bought it and read it. I discovered what more than five hundred thousand readers have learned. When a woman's mother is snatched from her, in my case when I was thirty-two and my mother was sixty, the hole she leaves behind never entirely fills up again.

"Losing my mother wasn't just a fact about me. It was the core of my identity, my very state of being," Hope writes in the introduction to the 2006 edition of *Motherless Daughters*. She has written three more books about mothers and daughters since the first edition came out in 1994, is married and now a mother herself of two girls, Maya and Eden. Now living in Topanga Canyon, California, Hope writes a letter to herself a few years after her mother's death.

*

Dear Hope,

I see you, through the dim tunnel of memory, sitting at the round dining table in your off-campus apartment. It's winter of your sophomore year, 1984. You've got the apartment to yourself, your roommates still in class for another hour. They're your family of sorts now, these two brilliant, sweet, eccentric women. Soon they'll come bursting through the front door, windmills of action and noise, stamping snow from their boots and shrugging off their woolen coats, and you'll all retire to the kitchen to wok a dinner for three. But right now, it's just you and the rooms of pockmarked hardwood floor, the secondhand upholstered furniture, the row of Joni Mitchell and Janis Joplin albums lined up next to the turntable.

A bitterly cold January wind is skidding off Lake Michigan, and as usual the heat in your building is turned up too high. You've had to lift the wooden windows a few inches to equalize the room. A thin stream of chilled air trickles in at waist level, and the steam radiator in the living room clangs and hisses in the background. Every eight minutes the El train rumbles by a half block away, making the walls tremble.

This is what you will miss most when you leave here: the warmth, the predictability, the safety that comes from belonging to a place and knowing what comes next. You will look for this kind of security always, the kind you had as a child when your family was still a closed circle unbroken by death.

Sometimes you will find it. Sometimes you will not.

Of course, you don't know this yet. Right now, you're pecking with intense focus at the keyboard of your blue Smith-Corona electric typewriter, working on an application for a summer internship at *Outside* magazine, and you're convinced that your professional future depends on how this letter is received.

This is how you think at nineteen: black or white, everything or nothing, unprecedented success or total failure. Everything matters, *so much*, every action, every word. You measure out your speech in careful doses, obsessing over sentences that came out too fast or sounded wrong. You plan every move in advance, meticulously and carefully. *Control*—that's what it will later come to be called. You will embrace control, because control leaves little room for unexpected shifts for which you are neither ready nor prepared. The world cannot tilt off its axis if you have not allowed room for it to happen. This is what you believe.

Control minimizes risk, which feels like a good idea now. Only much later will you discover the downside to this, that the fullest parts of life unroll as the result of impulsive choices. You will think you're taking a risk when you move to Tennessee after college, and later when you go to graduate school with no clear idea of how you'll pay for it, but really, these are small ones. You will shy away from big risks because you'll think you're lacking courage. This is not true. Courage, you have plenty of. What you're missing is faith. Faith in something other than yourself. Faith in . . . well, to rely on a word that's going to become excessively overused, the *universe*. Faith that whatever happens, you will nonetheless survive.

A phone call is coming from your father in a few weeks that's going to send you into a spin. He's going to say he's done with being a single parent; it's too much stress, too hard, and he's packing his bags to leave, sending your brother and sister to live with your grandmother. You will tell him, with a ferocity you didn't know you have, so help you God if he leaves those kids you'll make sure he never sees them again. He will stay. Twenty years later, a shaman in Malibu will tell you this was the moment when part of your soul left your body, and she will try to put it back. You will wonder if she's full of shit, but part of you will know she's right: You will feel your sense of trust leaving with that phone call like vapor lifting from your body.

What you will feel inside is true: No one is standing on the shore to toss you a life preserver if you start to drown. What you don't yet know is that for the rest of your life, with uncanny timing, a buoy will always appear when you need one: the offer of a bed to sleep in, a ride from a stranger, a check for $425 that arrives in the mail the same day you receive an unexpected $420 bill. This kind of synchronicity will occur again and again, as if relentlessly trying to prove its point, but twenty years will have to pass before you figure out what's going on.

Twenty years is a long time. So I am here to tell you:
Try to find faith now. You are not a random peg. There is a
hole where you fit in this world, a place uniquely molded
just for you. Everything you do does matter—but both
more and less than you think. Your good choices will
please you, but they will not redeem you. Your mistakes
will hurt, but they will not cripple you. You are both more
resourceful than you think and more protected than
you know.

So take risks. Take them now. The man you're going to
meet next year, the pre-law student who loves books and
maps and you? You're not going to marry him, though you
won't ever regret loving him. Still, you might as well join
the Peace Corps after graduation, fly off to Niger or
Micronesia, instead of taking a job near him. You'll need
the life experience to write about later, but don't write a
Peace Corps memoir, *please*—there will be far too many
of those. Sell your car, buy a one-way plane ticket, work
your way across Europe. Don't worry about running out of
money. If you do, you'll figure out how to manage. Write
short stories in your free time. So what if they suck? I
mean it: really, so what? Stick with it. You'll get better
with time.

Everything you're worried about won't happen without
careful planning and constant vigilance—the husband,
the children, the house—will all eventually come. Your
siblings will do better than just survive. They will thrive.
Your father's health will hold out for another twenty years.
The next few years are yours for the living. Because, let's
face it, you're not going to up and go trekking through the
Himalayas when you've got two kids and a teaching job

and an unruly house that keeps breaking down. Start meditating and doing yoga soon; it'll save you twenty years of anxiety. Sleep with a woman now, so you don't have to wonder about it later. Try peyote with your roommates instead of always being the designated driver. Follow the Grateful Dead for a summer for no reason other than the music is pretty good and the people seem sort of interesting. Get a tattoo. Dye your hair, just because you feel like a change. *Whatever.* In the end, your GPA and your resume aren't going to matter. Raw talent and discipline will. Just get yourself to Iowa City by 1990 because that's where everything starts clicking into place. The time between now and then is yours for the living. If only you can stop being so afraid.

I know your fear, even better than you do. Who could understand it more than I? I know how many things there are to be afraid of: breast cancer, airplane crashes, homelessness, religious fanatics, orphanhood, AIDS. I know how huge and overwhelming the fear can be, and how planning out every detail makes it contract. But one day you'll learn that fear comes from a projection of what might be, what could be, what better not be, instead of what is. *What is* is now. *What is* is you. And you're too buoyant to drown.

Lean back. Trust the water. I know it's hard. But the current will carry you safely to places you can't even imagine. Don't worry. Really: don't worry. Let go.

Float, baby. Float,
Hope

· ✳ ·

CATERINA FAKE

Founder of Flickr

"You're a real pain in the ass."

$\mathcal{A}$VERAGE students take heart. Caterina Fake, cofounder of Flickr, a photo-sharing Web site that was reportedly sold to Yahoo for nearly $30 million in 2005, says she had terrible grades in middle and high school. "If you looked at me during those years, you would have thought 'Caterina is doomed to mediocrity,'" she says. "Even my parents thought I was going to be a failure."

It's not hard to see how her parents might have formed this idea. When Caterina was in kindergarten, she hated wearing shoes. She threw them, hid them, anything she could do to avoid putting them on. Needless to say, getting Caterina ready for her Montessori school each day was like waging a small war. Finally, one day her mother decided to send her to school without her shoes. The shoeless, insubordinate kindergartener arrived at school and persuaded all the other kids to throw their shoes out the window . . . where it was raining. Bam! Caterina was suspended for two days.

She was not just a defiant kid, she was a defiant, *smart* kid, which gave her rebelliousness a devilish twist. Bored in middle school she often skipped classes. The principal and guidance counselor insisted that she had to attend, so she complied—

with a vengeance. She read all the class assignments, as well as the sources in the bibliography so that she could pepper her teachers with questions they didn't know the answers to.

"These poor teachers. I was beastly to them," she said. "I would say, 'Well if you happened to read this seminal text in your field you'd know this.'" Finally her teachers told Caterina that if she felt the need to skip class, they wouldn't report her.

Caterina's inner picture of herself never suffered, despite the poor academic record she was compiling. She preferred to be off doing her own thing. And her work wasn't necessarily bad, but it wasn't presented in a way that would earn her a good grade. Still, looking back she believes she could have benefited from understanding earlier in life that brainpower and work cannot stand alone. "The thing that makes people happy and successful is the ability to work with other people—the social skills," she explained.

Eventually Caterina caught on, big-time. Flickr's secret sauce, in fact, was its ability to let users socialize through photographs. The site, which has a user base of four million, turned Caterina into a public figure. She was on *Time's 100 Most Influential People in the World* list in 2006. She is also a highly regarded Web guru and a widely read blogger.

But life has slowed since her daughter, Sonnet Beatrice Butterfield, was born in 2007. "Having a baby changes your pace, and I've been slowing down to an extent I never did before. I'm paying more attention to my inner life," she said. If there's any justice, Sonnet will *really* like wearing shoes, going to class, getting good grades, and being nice. Here Caterina writes to herself at eleven.

*

Hey Kid,

Listen. You're pretty smart. An optimistic, cocksure smarty-pants. A firecracker and a prodigy. But guess what? You're eleven years old, and you just haven't seen much of the world. Take it from me, there's a lot you don't know yet, and I'm here to pass on some hard-won wisdom got by living life with its concomitant hard knocks.

Why should you listen to me? I'm not some "authority figure" you will feel compelled to resist, since authority-resisting is your particular area of expertise. "Yeah, yeah," you say, waving your hand, rolling your eyes. "Pfft. Whatever with you." But listen, the reason you should listen to me is, I'm you. You. Got it? Good.

So you're awesome, brilliant, and bold. You know all that. But I'm here to tell you—you're a real pain in the ass. You're a brat! You're going to look back and feel bad about all those teachers, principals, guidance counselors, deans, and professors you tormented. You're going to want to say you're sorry to them. They're just people. Folks. And you're going to learn kindness and compassion that you don't think you need at eleven.

Sure it's fun putting one over on the grown-ups. But believe me, in the future there will be many times you'll wish you'd been nicer to them rather than tougher or craftier or cleverer. Being smart isn't all there is. You'll learn later on that having friends and allies will do you a lot more good than having people who resent you or find you annoying. And you'll evolve into a kinder, gentler Caterina. Who'd'a thought?

Just cool it, OK? You don't have to prove anything to anyone. Be nicer sooner. You won't ever regret it, not once.

Cheerio!
You (aka Me)

P.S. You're not going to get into Yale. Them's the breaks, kid. But you'll have a great life anyway, I promise.

. ✳ .

Julie Foudy

World Cup and Olympic Soccer Player

"Laughter is mandatory."

SHE'S LOUD. She's a leader. And she's a massively talented soccer player. But one thing Julie Foudy refused to be was Little Bo Peep. As a little girl, she was such a diehard tomboy that on the day she was supposed to play the girlie role of Little Bo Peep she showed up at her elementary school in an Izod-brand shirt and shorts. "Apparently I just threw a fit about putting on a dress," says Julie, recalling the family story.

Talking to Julie, I couldn't help but feel that she would be one of the greatest pals I could ever have if our worlds overlapped. She is easy going and accepting, so much so that it was hard to spot the grit that fueled her extraordinary eighteen-year stretch as a midfielder on the U.S. Women's National Team, thirteen of which she spent as a captain. She is a two-time World Cup champion, as well as a two-time Olympic gold medalist (in 1996 and 2004) and a 2000 Olympic silver medalist.

Nope, there really was no need to put on a dress. Since retiring in 2004, Julie has been inducted into the National Soccer Hall of Fame (with teammate Mia Hamm), played a pivotal role in preserving Title IX, and with her husband,

Ian Sawyers, launched the Julie Foudy Sports Leadership Academy in 2006. A summer camp that fosters leadership roles for girls ages twelve to eighteen, it now operates in three locations. She works full time for ESPN and is also a popular public speaker.

Growing up, Julie never questioned her love of soccer. Still, the athleticism that was so obvious on the field brought complications once she reached Mission Viejo High School in California. She wore her curly hair short because she feared that it would spread out horizontally, rather than hang vertically, if she let it grow. Her hair and her still-boyish figure caused confusion. "People would call me 'young man' or 'boy.' I was devastated by that. I would wear these big old hoop earrings, trying to show that I was not a boy—that I could be feminine and still be athletic," Julie remembers.

At thirty-seven, Julie recollects this time with special poignancy now that girls are a bigger part of her life than ever before. In addition to the young women in her camps, she welcomed her first child, Isabel (aka Izzy), into her life in January of 2007. "She has a chill personality. She's always smiling," reports the new mother. Here is Julie's letter to her younger self as a freshman in high school.

*

Dear Jules,

You are never going to look like them, and who the heck cares?! Yeah, I see you constantly looking at that "cool crowd" and wondering why you don't fit in. You are different—thank goodness. You have concave boobs, short, thick hair, and are an athlete. Just keep wearing those big hoop earrings so the checkers at the grocery store stop calling you "little boy."

But looks are temporary; your strengths are not. You are funny, strong, confident, smart, and full of passion.

Your short, moppy hair is temporary (even if you're convinced that growing it out means it will grow *wide* instead of long). Your passion to make a difference in life is not.

Feeling awkward is temporary. Your desire to excel academically is not. Concave boobs are temporary (lie). Your love for competing and sweating is not. Wanting to fit in is temporary. The joy you feel when you run around on a grassy field is not.

So Jules, stop looking over there, and instead start thinking about how *free* you feel when you are surrounded by your teammates. Laughter surrounds you all. They will teach you some of the greatest lessons in life. They will teach you that you have to believe before you can achieve. They will teach you about treating others with respect. They will teach you that your dreams aren't crazy but are, in fact, courageous. They will teach you about caring more than others think is wise and expecting more than others think is possible.

Most important, they will teach you that laughter is permitted. Scratch that. Laughter is *mandatory.* So remember to laugh, and laugh often. After all, this is that oh-so-beautiful stage in our teenage lives that we all go through. Yeah, even those cool girls who look so perfectly made up—they feel awkward as well. I promise you, it doesn't last.

So go put on that padded bra, and fake it 'til you make it.

God hates chickens, so giddy up. Woooohooooo!

Jules

· ✳ ·

PHOTO: NoahHamiltonPhoto.com

BETHANY HAMILTON

Professional Surfer

"Your shot at being a champion
will be wide open."

THERE IS no mystery in Bethany Hamilton's mind about how she survived losing her arm to a fourteen-foot tiger shark on Halloween morning in 2003 while she was surfing in Kauai, Hawaii. "It was Jesus Christ who gave me peace when I got attacked by the shark," she writes. The thirteen-year-old got back to the beach and was rushed to the hospital where her father was scheduled to have knee surgery that day. Bethany ended up taking her father's place in the operating room.

What is inconceivable to most of us has been folded into the Hamilton family's life like a key ingredient of a life of faith and purpose. Devout Christians, the Hamiltons are also a surfing family who recognized Bethany's talent early on. By the time she was seven, she could catch and surf waves without her parents being in the water. Bethany's drive to surf was astonishingly undiminished by the trauma of the shark attack. She got back into the water with a board only three weeks after the attack and made it to the finals of the 2004 NSSA World Championship just eight months later.

She suffered the inevitable lurches of adjusting to her changed body, but the trauma does not rule her life. "I often dream that I have both my arms again, and I wake up expecting the whole shark business to be a nightmare. But it's not. It's my reality now, and I've learned to accept it. I've moved on," she said.

As inspirational as this story is, and as tidy as its conclusion seems to be, it is far from over, as Bethany has pointed out. Two things have become very clear to her. Her fundamental dream is undiminished: She has made it into the pro ranks of surfing and wants to win there. And she wants to channel her experience into inspiration for others, without being preachy.

So, she has created a personal documentary called *Heart of a Soul Surfer*, which has been shown at multiple film festivals and at hundreds of churches. She has produced an autobiography called *Soul Surfer*, a conversation with teens and 'tweens called *Devotions for the Soul Surfer*, and has more books in the works.

Bethany's story will soon reach millions. A movie about her remarkable experience will be "wide released" in theaters around the world in 2008. The story has all the drama and beauty that Hollywood craves—with the irresistible magnetism of a true story and a happy ending.

Now eighteen, Bethany travels around the world on surfing expeditions and competitions and on missions for World Vision, a charitable organization benefiting children. She writes to herself at about the time she turned thirteen, the spring before the shark attack.

*

Hey Bethany!

You dream of one thing only: becoming a world champion surfer. This is why you get up at dawn, don't eat hamburgers and pizza (as much as you'd *love* to), and run five miles a day. At thirteen you are so sure that winning the World Championship Tour is in your future that sometimes all you want to do is fast-forward into that moment.

But this year you're going to deal with some unimaginable challenges, and your life is totally going to change. You'd just laugh in disbelief if I told you. So here is what I wish you could think of. First, your willingness to be led by God will help you through what is ahead. You will pray to be of use to Him and you will find that you can be, beyond what you'd expect or even imagine.

Second, what happens this year will seem to wipe away your dream of becoming a champion. Many people may question your goal. But do not let it go. You will find tremendous fortitude and ability—and with God's help and the help of special friends in your life, you will become one of the top twenty-five surfers in the pro world by the time you are eighteen.

Your shot at being a champion will be wide open, even when you are contending with conditions never faced by any other surfer.

As overwhelming as events will be, remember that getting to the other side of them will bring a cascade of new opportunities into your life. You can be a surfer and at the same time inspire others by sharing your story about how you've overcome adversity.

Whenever a storm blows into your life—big or small—remember to read Jeremiah 29:11—you'll understand later!

Never give up!

Love,
Future Bethany :)

· ✳ ·

Mýa Harrison

Singer/Songwriter

"Invent your own definition of success."

"*I* STOPPED raising my hand in eighth grade," says Mýa Harrison, the singer and Grammy Award winner, about her middle school years in Maryland. A top student, she got tired of being criticized when she raised her hand to answer a teacher's question or got an A on a test. With bushy hair, a scrawny frame, and excellent grades, Mýa was a loner in middle school.

Her salvation was participating in music and dance outside of school. From ages twelve to eighteen she was part of a multicultural performance group. The kids improvised their own routines, performing at high-profile venues such as The Kennedy Center. "We were all there to perform and perfect ourselves, not focused on appearance or materialistic things," recalls Mýa. "It was very healthy."

Since her first self-titled hit CD, *Mýa*, went platinum with three, top ten singles when she was eighteen, Mýa has released three more: *Fear of Flying*, *Moodring*, and *Liberation*. When we spoke, her single "Ridin" was a fixture on the radio—and also the inspiration for a YouTube-based contest. Contestants were invited to submit a thirty-second video, describing themselves, their interests, and why Mýa might want to go "ridin" with them on a date. Hundreds of men uploaded their videos, displaying the full spectrum of what men think is attractive about themselves.

As gratifying as it has been, the fast-paced development of her career made her feel adrift. But after moving back to her roots in the Washington, DC, area a few years ago, Mýa bought a house, built a recording studio, and, newly centered, has been exploring fresh areas of creative expression. In addition to assembling a band, she's appeared in movies, including *Chicago Havana Nights, Shall We Dance, Metrosexual, Ways of the Flesh, Cover*, and *Bottleworld*. She's put teaching back in her life, too, by starting the Mýa Arts & Technology Foundation in 2005. The not-for-profit is charged with providing an arts education to DC's inner-city youth. Mýa continues to teach dance and sound engineering classes every summer.

From meek social outcast to object of desire, today's Mýa would seem to have nothing in common with the middle-schooler she was. But she says it's only in the last three years or so that she has fully realized the wisdom of the message in her letter to the young Mýa—and still finds it applicable in her everyday life.

*

Dear ReRe,

They call you "Tree" because your hair is so extraordinarily bushy. When you sit in the front of a classroom, your hair blocks the view of the blackboard for the students sitting behind you. You have braces. You're underdeveloped. You speak properly. You're completely intimidated by the conversations some girls have about boys.

You are so isolated that you don't even sit at lunch with a regular group of kids. You prefer to skip lunch and go to the library.

The measure of your heartache, that deep desire to be accepted, is a secret you are keeping. You have a single Guess logo patch that you removed from a pair of Guess jeans. Every night you snip it off of the jeans you wore that day and sew it on to another pair.

You've been criticized for not having brand-name clothes, so you are doing the only thing you can to look like you do. Guess jeans are like gold at school. They may not be the ticket to popularity, or even acceptance, but wearing that logo is like wearing a magic shield that will protect you from at least some of the arrows that kids would have hurled at you. The logo is protection.

I want to tell you that it is okay to be an individual. All of your life people are going to criticize you. If it's not your hair, it's your teeth. If it's not the way you speak, it's your background. When you hear one comment consistently from a group, it's natural to want to change yourself. But this can be a trap.

Please, invent *your* own definition of success because it varies for everyone. And please, Mýa, define what beautiful is to *you*. Because you'll drive yourself crazy trying to fit someone else's idea of beauty. You'd be living life held hostage to a standard that you can never meet or that always changes—just like you're being held hostage by a brand of jeans right now.

Know that you are loved by the people who matter forever. Keep gazing out your window every night into the universe, and remind yourself there is something greater than all of us. Focus on and reach for the stars and, I promise you, you'll be one too.

From the friend you don't know inside of you,
Mýa, formerly known as "Tree"

· ✳ ·

MAUREEN KELLY

Founder of tarte cosmetics

*"I want so desperately to
shake you from this nightmare."*

ON PAPER, Maureen Kelly, founder of tarte cosmetics, sounds like a hard-driving MBA with a perfect business plan. She launched her company in 1999, in the shadow of giants like Estée Lauder, Avon, and L'Oréal. In 2001, tarte's double-ended lip glosses made Oprah's famous "O List." Its gel cheek stains have been voted Best Gel Blush by *InStyle* magazine for six years in a row. *Entrepreneur* magazine and OPEN from American Express named Maureen 2006 Woman of the Year, and her company ranked No. 944 in the Inc. 5000 list. By 2007 her company had annual revenues estimated at $20 million, and her products were being sold at Sephora, QVC, and Henri Bendel, among other retailers.

All of this was *not* part of the plan, however. Maureen, a feisty, redheaded, thirty-five-year-old, had been headed toward a career in psychology. After stints as a buyer at Lord and Taylor and an assistant for an interior designer, she earned a master of arts in school psychology at the New School for Social Research, a master of arts in clinical psychology at Columbia University, and was also pursuing a doctorate there. "But I just wasn't feeling fulfilled," she remembers.

Her husband, Mark, encouraged her to chase her improbable dream of starting a makeup line. "Everyone thought I was crazy because I wasn't a makeup artist," she says. But with Mark's support—and their life savings—she launched tarte in the one-bedroom apartment they shared in New York City.

That was in 1999. Two years later, Maureen was awoken by a call from Mark, who worked as a bond trader at Keefe, Bruyette & Woods in the World Trade Center. She never thought their morning conversation would be their last.

Today, in the life she didn't plan, Maureen is remarried and the mother of a sixteen-month-old. When we spoke, she was pregnant with her second child, who was due in December of 2007. Her letter is to herself at twenty-nine when this future—actually any future—was unimaginable in the months after Mark died.

Maureen,

I can see you now, standing in line at the triage center amid the chaos of screaming sirens and flashing red lights, slowly suffocating on the thick haze of smoke that has already begun to permeate your soul. I can see the expression on your face, the deadening of the eyes as the light slowly fades from within you. I want so much to huddle beside you as I watch your freckled, nail-bitten finger move down the list of names, searching. . . .

I can see the hesitation in your steps as you return in the black of night to the apartment you once shared together—the shudder when you are greeted only by the interminable echo of the slamming door. I can see the vacant stare as you scan the cardboard boxes filled with cosmetics stacked almost to the ceiling in every corner of the room—remnants of hope from what now seems like another lifetime. I see you slowly rifle through one such box and finger a compact that you somehow convinced him to press with his large, calloused, rugby-player hands. Though he complained vociferously, all the while a boyish grin played on his lips. He could do nothing to disguise his pride.

I can see you now, surrounded by your family as they try in vain to shelter you from the specter of grief that haunts you. I can see your apprehension and uncertainty as they counsel you to sell the company, to acknowledge the additional stress you burden yourself with each and every day as you stubbornly cling to this fleeting dream— a dream they fear will only remind you of Mark's absence. As though, even for a fraction of a second, you could forget.

I can see you, Maureen; I can see you through all of this. I watch as you stumble blindly through the fog of these years, never daring to hope for anything beyond survival. And I want so desperately to shake you from this nightmare and offer you even the smallest glimpse of a future you could never imagine. I want to tell you of the strength that still resides in the deepest recesses of your soul and will emerge once again. I want to whisper to you of the hope that refuses to be shrouded in darkness and will prevail. I want you to once again laugh as I remind you of your spontaneity, obstinacy, and astounding capacity to love without boundaries.

How I wish you could see yourself as I see you now. How I wish I could share a glimpse of this woman as she defies the expectations of all those around her and slowly transforms those haphazard piles of cosmetics strewn around her one-bedroom apartment into a multimillion-dollar company called tarte.

Maureen, I wish you could see this woman now, and the gentle and patient companion walking beside her. The man whose disarming Southern charm and flashing blue eyes finally give her the courage to dare to love again. I wish you could feel the tenderness in his caress, his ability to wake the passion she believed had withered years ago. I wish you could feel just the slightest hint of his gentle breath on her cheek as he whispers to her in the darkness, reminding her that she is not alone.

How I want you to know the scent of her baby boy as she buries her head in his pale hair—inhaling every inch of him. I want you to feel his chubby fingers clinging to the nape of her neck and to see how he stares at her with those deep brown eyes framed by boy curled lashes. I wish you could rejoice in the sound of his squealing laughter, the unadulterated joy of his shrieks. How I wish I could take that trembling hand, Maureen, and place it on the belly of this woman as she once again swells with the promise of new life.

With so much love,
Mo

. ✳ .

Vida Zaher Khadem

Filmmaker/Painter

"This is how you unshackle yourself."

OF ALL the compelling, vivid stories Vida Zaher Khadem, filmmaker and artist, can tell about her life as an Afghan emigrant, the most poignant is about doing her homework as a sixth grader. Having left Kabul by traveling across the mountains with backpacks to Pakistan in 1981 because of the Russian invasion, Vida's family settled in New Delhi for three years. Then her mother got a job in the United States as an international broadcaster for Voice of America.

The family moved to Washington, DC, and Vida attended a school where she was the only nonblack student. "They called me white, but of course I didn't even know English and knew nothing of U.S. culture," says Vida. She was picked on constantly: basketballs thrown at her during gym class, the chair taken from her desk, pushes in the hallway. "In the beginning, the only mean English words I could say to defend myself were 'you're stupid.' So that's all I would say over and over" when they bullied her.

If she faced enormous odds socially at school, it was just as daunting at home with her books. Having always been an excellent student and knowing that her father expected perfection, Vida remembers spending eight to ten hours per night on her homework. She knew so little English that she used a dictionary to tediously decipher the assignments. Frequently she looked up a word's meaning only to have to then look up the words used in the definition. Through sheer perseverance, she learned and, amazingly, brought home a report card of As, Bs, and one C. "When my dad looked at it and saw the C, he just threw the report card back at me," recalls Vida.

After a year in the city, Vida's family moved to Virginia, where she lived under her parents' strict supervision until her mid-twenties. She was not allowed to be out after dark. She was never permitted to sleep overnight at a friend's, or even at a relative's, house. When it came time for her to go to college, her father did not want her to live in a dorm, so she commuted to George Mason University.

The Afghan culture's ultra-conservative values were partly to blame. But her father's apprehension of American culture was responsible too. "My father was extremely fearful of what might happen to his daughters. Would they get pregnant? That's what it looked like when he watched the daytime talk shows," says Vida. She counts herself lucky that both of her parents were well educated and considered schooling their daughters of the utmost importance, an attitude that contrasts sharply to that of most Afghans.

Friendless for almost all of those middle and high school years, Vida remembers living in a very narrow corridor: home, school, home, homework. Even at home the isolation was intense because each member of the family was struggling with the enormous adjustment to their new country. Her sister was five years older and married after only a year. Her brother was not someone Vida felt she could confide in until she became an adult.

As Vida overcame the language barrier outside of home, a new one grew up inside of it. She was required to speak Dari to her parents, but her skill in that language stayed stuck at the third-grade level. So even as she matured and English became the language of her mind, she could communicate only rudimentary and simple ideas with her parents. "I don't know if they ever see me as an adult because I am always talking to them in this baby language," she says. Unable to talk about complicated topics, their understanding of each other suffered.

As she went through high school and into her first year of college, all of these difficulties intensified because she realized that she loved the arts—music, theater, dancing, painting. She felt joyful in those activities. But she was thwarted here, too, because of a cultural prohibition. "In the East, women who go into the arts are not well respected. Women who were smart and good became doctors, nurses, or teachers," explains Vida.

This is the unlikely background of the quiet-spoken, slender young woman with large soulful eyes who has already made three moving films. The first, *A Bleak Existence*, was a documentary on women living on the Afghanistan and Pakistan border. The second was *FireDancer*, a feature-length film about Afghan émigrés' experiences in America. Vida became the associate director and coproducer on the film when Jawed Wassel, the director and her mentor, was brutally murdered before the film was finished. *FireDancer* had its world premiere in Kabul's Ghazi Stadium, the site of many Taliban hangings and beheadings. A huge success in Afghanistan, *FireDancer* was the first and only film that country has ever submitted to the Academy Awards.

Vida's most recent film, *Return to Afghanistan*, is the most wrenching. Begun as a chronicle of her brother's return to

Kabul, the city he left so long ago, the film veers in a new direction when Vida and her crew return to New York and the terrorist attacks occur on 9/11. It was being shown as part of the United Nations Film Festival program when I met with Vida.

Now in her mid-thirties, she writes to herself in the first semester of her sophomore year at George Mason.

My dear Vida,

You feel like a prisoner draped in chains. The only things that bring you joy are your painting and the arts. You are studying biology. Your parents proudly say to all the relatives: "She's going to be a doctor." You have gazed at the arts section of George Mason's course catalog with such yearning. Now you are contemplating doing the unthinkable: telling your parents you can't be pre-med—you want to major in the arts instead.

This seems more impossible than all the other difficult moments in your life. You know how disappointed they will be. Saying these few simple words to your parents feels like an act of such unprecedented rebellion that it may bring down the sky.

But Vida, take heart. This is how you unshackle yourself, or at least it is the beginning. This is the first step of carving out an artist's life from meager raw materials. More important, it is the first step of extracting *you*, Vida, your real self, out of the expectations of your parents, the yoke of the Afghan culture, and your lonely experience as an immigrant.

She is in there, the real you. And Vida, she's brimming with talent. You will direct arresting films, create giant paintings, write a science fiction screenplay that is a love story. And though there are many trials to come . . . and heartbreak . . . at age thirty-four, you will feel unchained for the first time.

With faith in you,
Vida

. ✳ .

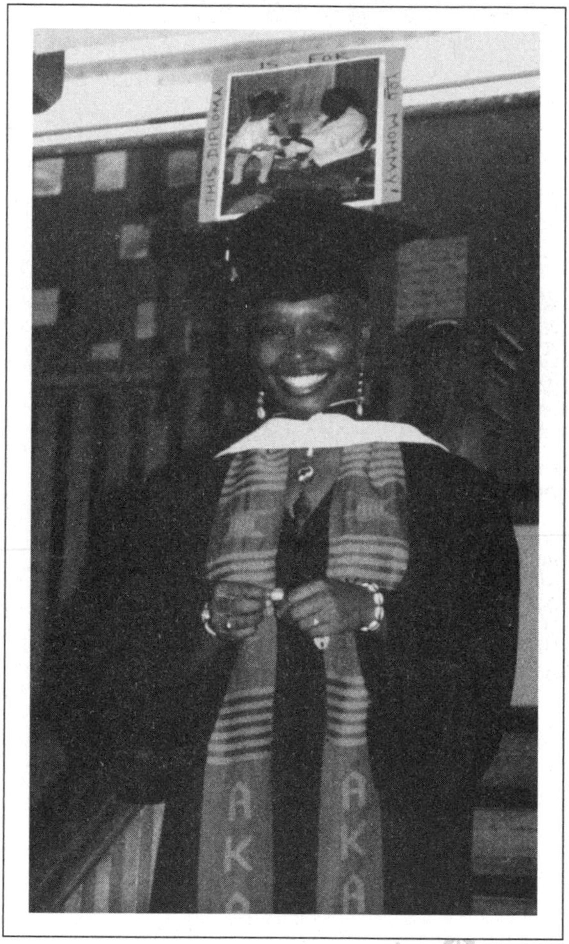
THIS DIPLOMA
MOMMY!
AKA

Monique King-Viehland

Executive Director, CCRC
New Jersey State Government

"The shame will fall away."

MONIQUE KING-VIEHLAND'S mother had a dream when her daughter was little. In the dream, God told her that some people are destined for greatness and others give birth to children who are destined for greatness. Monique's mom, who was raising two children by herself in Trenton, New Jersey, felt her destiny was the latter. So—you guessed it—Monique grew up believing she could do anything.

Monique is executive director of the Capital City Redevelopment Corporation, a New Jersey state agency charged with leading and coordinating redevelopment in downtown Trenton. Previously she was a special assistant to the deputy chief of staff for New Jersey's Governor John Corzine, focusing on community and economic development in Camden. Encouraged by her mother to think big, she recalls with a laugh some of her early ambitions. "In fourth grade I decided I wanted to go to summer camp in Vermont. We had never been outside of Trenton, New Jersey, and we didn't have any money. My mom said, 'We'll figure it out.'"

Being an African American striver set her up for criticism. Because she got good grades, ran for class president, and was voted most likely to succeed, Monique was accused of not being black enough at Ewing High School. She was one of the few black girls to be on both the mostly white football cheerleading squad and the mostly black basketball squad. "Oreo cookie" and "wannabe-white" rang in her ears more than once.

While the teasing cut deeply, Monique also lived with a tiny undercurrent of worry that she would be unmasked—that she *wasn't* good enough, that maybe she *couldn't* do everything, despite what her mother told her. This fear could ignite and be fanned into a roaring blaze by the sporadic appearance of her father, a crack cocaine drug addict who had split from her mother when Monique was two years old. Because she was so embarrassed by him, he was her secret. Most of her friends didn't know he existed.

But every once in a while he popped unexpectedly into her life. Monique, thirty, writes to herself on one of these occasions during her sophomore year, when she was at the Quaker Bridge Mall with a large group of her cheerleading buddies from the football squad.

Dear Monique,

You never know when he's going to come find you, and when he does, you never know how to make him go away. There you were with your friends, about to get a bite at Friendly's, when he showed up, stumbling. You tried to avoid him, to brush him off, and then he got belligerent and loud.

"What's wrong with you? *I'm your father!*"

The moment seems trapped in slow motion. Mall shoppers stopping and turning to look at the two of you. Your friends, puzzled, looking at him and then at you, especially when you called him Dad.

"It's okay, Dad."

Trying to get your friends to go on ahead without you . . . "I'll be fine."

It wasn't much better when they left. You spoke to him for a while, he stormed off, and after you stopped crying you rejoined your friends.

Awkward silence. You finally talked to them about him but it still feels like the end of the world. He is a sore spot, a vulnerable, undefended place on the armor you wear every day. You wonder, *Are people going to look at him and think that that's me? Are people going to look at him and think less of me?*

Today—and for years—you'll want to repudiate him. You worry that he represents some kind of weakness lying in wait inside of you, something that will rise up and ruin everything. But that's just because you are young and not yet truly confident that your successes belong to you.

You don't believe this now, but your father actually is defining you just as much as your mother is. But don't worry. He will define you without limiting you from reaching for what you want. He will shape the career you pursue and your focus on making urban communities healthy. That is a gift from him, the man who seems to have nothing to give.

Today you are ashamed of him. Someday you will stop seeing him as a threat to your dreams and you'll find the shame will fall away. You'll even understand that he actually does love you—he just can't act like someone who does because of his addiction.

You will make it,
Monique

· ✳ ·

SONYA KITCHELL

Singer/Songwriter

"What you don't have
will allow you to become something
that would have been impossible."

$\mathcal{H}$ER SONGS are filled with so much nuance and deliv-
ered with such artistry that it's a surprise to realize how young
Sonya Kitchell is. A week after her eighteenth birthday, I met
Sonya in Manhattan's East Village office of Velour, her manager and record label. She settled in with a cup of hot soup
and a handful of shopping bags filled with provisions for an
upcoming trip. She was about to embark on a month-long
tour of India with her father, Peter Kitchell, a world-renowned
poster artist and photographer.

Raised on forty acres near Northampton, Massachusetts, by
parents who were successful artists (her mother is Gayle
Kabaker, an illustrator and graphic designer), Sonya started
taking voice lessons at seven years old. She sang at the Special
Olympics at age ten and began playing jazz standards with a
band at thirteen. From the outside, it looks as though her
career grew steadily, with an explosive push from Starbucks
when her 2006 album, *Words Came Back to Me*, was the second
work featured in the company's Hear Music series. But to
Sonya it has all unfolded with an uncanny sense of timing.

"For my entire life and career I've been thrown into the fire just before I'm ready. When you are forced to do things that are a little scary, you should do them. I've seen again and again that I can do it," Sonya says.

This hiatus from touring allowed her to participate in family life for a few weeks rather than alight for the usual brief visit. She'd goofed around with Max, her precocious thirteen-year-old brother who likes to walk around in his bathrobe opining on the percentages of her income that Sonya should be giving him. And she had enjoyed a big birthday bash, attended by local friends as well as musicians and friends from across the country.

As we talked about the enormous change that she has experienced since she began touring on her own at sixteen, it became clear that this young woman's quiet demeanor cloaks high aspirations for herself in the decades to come. She hopes that in time her technical skill will give her a platform to help create change in the world. "I've always felt it was my duty to say something that was worth saying," she says.

Here is her letter to herself at fifteen, just as the touring began.

※

Dear Sonya,

I won't pretend that I have all the answers for you because here I am, only three years older than you are now. But I can give you a few hints about what's ahead. Your charmed life—the way it routinely delivers the perfectly thrilling and slightly scary next step for your career at exactly the right moment—will continue. At the same time, the contrast between those career leaps and the issues that bog you down will get more intense.

You're a child in an adult male world. Your mom has been with you much of the time, but now you're going on the road alone. You've had to grow up really quickly, taking on responsibilities that most people don't have until their twenties. But in return you get the euphoria of writing and performing your own work. On tour, you're sharing billing with Herbie Hancock, Rickie Lee Jones, and Aron Neville. You've gotten acquainted with performers like Jackson Brown and Tracy Chapman. You know that you have an almost unbelievable shot at stardom, so you made the difficult decision to leave high school to pursue it.

It's hard though, and it's going to get harder. It's like a yearning for the things a so-called normal life might have given you. A boyfriend. Going to high school. You feel embarrassed explaining that you occasionally work with a tutor to get your GED. People don't know that you were always a good student.

And the loneliness is going to be bad. There will be times when you are so, so tired and run down. You'll have to eat dinner alone because there's no one to eat it with. You'll start crying—then you're alone and crying. You'll have to cross the street, do a show, and pretend that everything is okay. Then, you're alone again in a hotel room.

You've never been the pretty, skinny girl—and you'll wish for that, off and on, for years. Sometimes the wish gets more intense because it's a harsh world for a performer. You don't want to have any flaw that people can tear you down with. You want to wrap yourself in that pretty-skinny package to protect yourself and give you the invincible confidence that a performer needs.

Nothing I say will stop these feelings you have. But I do know that incredible loneliness is incredibly normal for many people, whether they are at home with their family or on tour. And even though wishing for a boyfriend and a skinny body will continue, as time goes by you'll be more and more grateful for what you do have—and how what you *don't* have will allow you to become something that would have been impossible.

Not having or being everything you want will force you to become funny. Not having a million friends your own age will open the way for friendships with men and women aged thirty to sixty-five. Not going to high school will empower you to get your GED.

Not having a boyfriend . . . well, that's going to change. As a working, independent, constantly moving young woman, you'll learn to be with someone and let them go—while still feeling strong. You'll discover an ease and power that you had no idea was inside you.

Love,
Sonya

• * •

MINDY LAM

Founder of Mindy Lam Fine Crystal Jewelry

"Show your mom you will not fail."

$\mathcal{T}$O CALL Mindy Lam's creations "jewelry", doesn't do them justice. They're garlands that encircle a neck, trail down around the sternum, and hold a dinner-plate-sized flower. Or they are bendable wrist ropes. Or cascading blooms. Made of semi-precious stones, fresh water pearls, and Swarovski crystals, the imaginative, fantastical pieces are carried at Henri Bendel, the Philadelphia Museum of Art, and high-end boutiques—an impressive presence for a business that was launched only six years ago in 2002.

But that success is the smallest part of Mindy's remarkable story. She started life with two strikes against her. Born to a poor chicken farmer in the New Territory of Hong Kong, she entered the world in an unlucky year. And she was a first-born female, also considered unlucky. Custom, and her parents' friends, dictated that Mindy be given away, as her father's sister had been when she was born decades earlier. Remembering that day, her father would not allow it for Mindy.

Despite this decision, her father considered her unlucky and detached himself emotionally. Mindy was required to help her father mix the chicken feed, clean the pens, wash the eggs, and otherwise tend the family's thirty thousand chickens before and after school every day. Her younger sister and brother were spared such chores and treated lovingly. "When I was a teenager, I asked myself always why my sister and brother were better than me," remembers Mindy.

Despair began to engulf her between ages thirteen and sixteen. But two key turning points changed everything. One she describes in her letter. The other was a visit by a cousin who lived in the Washington, DC, area. "When he saw how hard I worked, he was in tears," says Mindy. He encouraged Mindy's mother and aunt to apply for the teenager to emigrate to the United States and live with him and his mother. In 1989, when she was twenty-one, she finally did.

Knowing only the scantiest English, she studied to get her hairdresser's license. She then spent eleven years gradually building her reputation and clientele in the DC area. Along the way she married briefly and had a daughter, Kelly, whom she sent to live with her mother in Hong Kong so that the girl would be brought up within a Chinese culture. While visiting Kelly in 2001, Mindy contracted necrotizing fasciitis, a rare bacterial disease, often called flesh-eating bacteria. Horribly painful, the disease almost caused Mindy to lose her feet to amputation.

During her nine months of recovery Mindy was bedridden, and her sister, Sindy, gave her some wire and crystal beads to occupy her. Mindy began creating her very first pieces. When she returned to the United States, she began wearing her handiwork, attracting the interest of her hair salon clients, who became her first customers.

The climactic scene of this Cinderella story took place in 2002 at Henri Bendel, where a jewelry buyer had invited the new jewelry maker to conduct a trunk show. Mindy not only avoided the hit-or-miss process of "auditioning" as a new vendor, but her work caught the eye of Bendel's president, Ed Burstell, during the trunk show. Within a month the Mindy Lam Collection was featured in a case. During her first year, retail sales at the store exceeded $190,000.

She now employs a dozen artisans in the United States and Hong Kong to help make the earrings, necklaces, brooches, and bracelets, which sell at prices ranging from $30 to $1,200. Mindy and her sister, Sindy, continue to personally handcraft the final pieces. Pricey as her couture collection is, almost anyone can afford one item. "I came from a poor family. I do not believe that only a rich person can enjoy Mindy Lam," she says.

Extremely grateful for where she finds herself today, Mindy's letter addresses herself at sixteen, when the first, most significant change in her life occurred.

Dear Miu Yee,
    You see your father treat your sister and brother so much better than you—and you wonder why.
    Why does nobody but your mom want you?
    Why do people have to tell you that you are an ugly girl?
    Why do you have to be so poor that you must wear other people's clothes?
    Why does your mother's rich family have to laugh at you and hold their noses when you are around?
    You have just about given up on yourself. You cry a lot. You skip school and don't really study anymore, even

though your father beats you for it. You refuse to listen to your mother and father. So now people are telling your father that you are dirt. "She is the kind of dirt that will never build a wall," they say. Nothing good could ever happen to you.

But today everything must change. Your mother sat down and talked. She told you that what you are going through is what she went through as a teenager, when she was abandoned by her step-grandmother. "When I see this, I do not see you as a bad kid," she said. "I do not want to leave you, but I do not want to continue my life if you continue what you are doing."

You were shocked. You both cried, and you told her, "Okay, Mom. It will be a wall. Whether I build a big wall or a building, I don't know, but I am telling you I will succeed." You said to yourself, *God, if you give me a chance, I will fight.*

Mindy, you have made a start. Do not hesitate about what is unknown. Success, it is difficult to make happen. But do not see anything as an obstacle. Look at it as climbing a mountain. Each mountain you climb will give you a better view. Show your mom you will not fail.

Your successful future self

· ✳ ·

DYLAN LAUREN

Founder of Dylan's Candy Bar

"You can't radiate loveliness
while worrying about whether your
shoes make your ankles look fat."

IN A FAMILY where understated aesthetics rule, where home is an all-white apartment, and your father is a fashion designer whose unerring eye for WASP-y chic has spawned a multi-billion-dollar empire, Dylan Lauren's admiration for goofy-looking bunny rabbits and Skittles' color palette seems inexplicable. But the thirty-one-year-old entrepreneur is doing exactly what her father, Ralph Lauren, did. Decades ago he saw potential—with the help of a giant dollop of fantasy—in a musty type of unfashionable clothing. She sees promise in putting familiar candy like Double Bubble Gum, Swedish Fish, and Gummy Bears on a pedestal—preferably one bedecked with peppermint swirls, set on a polkadot floor and lit by gumdrop-shaped pendant fixtures.

Dylan's Candy Bar, which opened in 2001 and hugs a well-placed corner on Third Avenue in Manhattan, lifts your spirits instantly. A candyland sensibility pulses here, but the vibe is fun, exuberant, and stylish rather than childish. "Candy has been a common thread throughout my whole life. I see it as art," she told me as we sat in her store's party room. It's obvious, once she says it. The room's wall and ceiling wear stripes in seven colors and are lit from behind. Consider also the scale of the lollipop tree, which sports suckers with a three-foot diameter, the hardware-store orderliness of paint pail containers for gumballs and the urbanity of Chinese-style take-out containers, which hold candy corn.

The idea: The Candy Girl deserves the kind of packaging and retail home that's as well-designed as other favorite shopping spots. But it has to be fun, that's the rule. Dylan, who still allows herself a daily ration of candy (red Swedish Fish, marshmallows, and red licorice laces are favorites), has since opened five stores in four other cities and is scouting for locations in Los Angeles, Las Vegas, London, and Japan.

Slender and fit, Dylan has inherited her father's olive complexion, which made her look tan even though we were just beginning to slog our way out of winter when we met. She has a long, slightly wild mane of chestnut hair and absolutely no pretensions. Wearing a hoodie and black track pants, she talked about what it was like to be fifteen when she began to think about her body—and how it was perceived by guys. The standards for beauty, stiff enough to meet for an ordinary, media-saturated adolescent, were particularly unreachable in Dylan's world.

"The models for my dad were my age. I always knew I was attractive, but there I was—surrounded by perfection. I was comparing myself to girls who became top models, not just to a pretty girl in my high school," she remembers. What's more, her fashion-conscious family *always* commented on beautiful girls. Here she writes to herself about her teenage body.

*

Dear Dill Pickle,

Am I fat?

Would he like me better if I were thinner?

She looks so much better than me in shorts!

Dylan, these are the thoughts and questions swirling
through your head these days. You're *not* fat. But you're
muscular. All those years of being a tomboy. Then sports:
track, volleyball, tennis, and swimming. Your biggest
worry was trying to become captain of the tennis team,
but now you care more about guys and how they'll react
to you.

It's fashion week in New York City, the *big* week for
your family. It feels confusing and mysterious. Why aren't
you like the lean, skinny girls you see up there on the
catwalk—and everywhere else at camp and in school? Is
it because you're an athlete? Because of genetics? Even
Mom is thin.

How your body looks seems crucially linked to how
attractive guys think you are.

Understand that you can change your body. You're not
stuck with what you've got. It's not a mystery. Right now
you're eating too much bread and carbohydrates—
including candy—and no protein. You know how Mom
says it took her time to grow into her shape and shed the
baby fat? That's because she, as you will too, has figured
out the equation: how much exercise and what kind,

along with how much food and what kind, it takes to
be healthy and lean. You just have to educate yourself.

The biggest part of that education should be this:
There are models who weigh one hundred pounds who
are miserable because they want to weigh ninety-five
pounds. Changing your body through diet and training
should not be an exercise in relentless self-criticism.
It should be an act of gratitude.

Your body serves you so well on tennis and volleyball
courts and on the track. Love it. Enjoy how beautiful it is
right now, because, trust me, looking back at you from
this age, I know that it is beautiful. Women have such
a short time to be attractive.

They say that beauty is wasted on youth because of
exactly what you are going through. You're too
embarrassed about every minor flaw and too attentive to
other girls' minor advantages. The real enemy of beauty
is self-consciousness. I know it sounds impossible, but
try to put it aside. You can't radiate loveliness while
worrying about whether your shoes make your ankles
look fat.

With Understanding,
The Candy Girl

· ✳ ·

DANY LEVY

Founder of *DailyCandy*

"Life is not a performance sport."

WHAT DO juice cleanses, a Japanese eyelash perm, and a clairvoyant-for-hire have in common? They all hit the selective radar of *DailyCandy*, a free daily email that beams unessential, but deliciously fun-to-know bulletins about new restaurants, fashion, beauty, and the arts to your inbox or phone. Now available in eleven U.S. cities as well as London, *DailyCandy* has three million subscribers across the globe and is routinely hailed as one of the few Internet companies launched during the dot-com boom that is an unqualified winner.

For Dany Levy, *DailyCandy's* founder, the company's success, recently underscored by a round of financing valuing it at $130 million, represents a key turning point. Proud as she is of what she's accomplished at a young age, she senses it's time to stretch herself in new ways. "I grew up overachieving. It's only now, at thirty-five, that I'm asking myself what I want—and trying to stop thinking about my life as the sum of my accomplishments on paper," she says.

Her bag of achievements started swelling in high school, where she admits she was one of those girls who would've been easy to hate. "Yeah," she says ruefully, "I ran with the 'cool' girls' crowd. Yuck. The whole thing was straight out of the movie *Heathers*." She was also smart, which earned her the nicknames "Bio Geek" and "Poetry Nerd."

In her senior year, Dany was accepted early to Brown University. But, eager to please her parents who prodded her to "just send her applications in and see what happens . . . ," she applied to Harvard, Yale, and Stanford as well. Stanford and Yale accepted her. She narrowed down the decision to Brown, which had a creative writing program, and Yale, because, well, it was Yale. Lured by the cachet and the accolades from her parents, she chose Yale but transferred after her freshman year to Brown. Her letter is to herself at Yale when she was eighteen.

*

Dear Dany,

   What is it with this need to always feel that you have to perform to be loved? You think that as long as you do this "good" girl stuff, if you keep all these plates spinning, you're guaranteed acceptance? How did the idea get wired in your head that if you get a zit or a B-plus or a roll of fat on your tummy, the world is most likely going to dump you flat on your ass?

   Listen, life is not a performance sport. You've been raised to think that credentials—the right college, the right hair, the right clothes, the good grades—are emotional currency. You've always believed, *Do the right thing, strive for perfection*, and you'll be happy, you'll be loved. But that is ultimately your Achilles heel. Though

some would call these attributes a blessing,
your need to be "good" all the time is stopping you
from listening to what *you*, Dany, really want.
Where is it written that you have to earn love and
approval? Do you think you won't get it otherwise?
Is plain old Dany—without the show-and-tell list of
accomplishments—loveable?
Why wouldn't she be?
You've zigzagged your way through this silly slalom
course of constantly trying to prove your worth, your right
to exist, and pleasing others. Why can't you see that
Dany, at her very essence, is your saving grace? You went
to Yale even though you wanted the creative writing
program at Brown because you and your parents liked the
sound of it. *Yale.*
Now you are correcting the course, by transferring to
Brown (Oh, as if that is such a bold move . . . . I know it
feels like one, but come now—you really have to extricate
yourself from that mode of thinking.) Time and time again
you will repeat this: start in a cookie-cutter, play-by-the-
book direction and then take a gutsy alternate path,
which will bring you your greatest successes and
satisfaction.
So a bit of advice. Keep it up—but do more of the
stuff that meets no one's criteria but your own. You
know how to identify the signs. It, whatever "it" you're
contemplating, probably scares you a little, befuddles
friends and family a little . . . but if you feel right about
it and it gives you that creative twitter in your stomach
when you think about it, do it.

Don't be so concerned about what the world thinks of you. Follow your instincts. You know damn well you really like that girl with the bad-ass streak. Let her out. She has some pretty neat things to say.

Dany

· ✳ ·

LISA LOEB

Singer/Songwriter/Actress

"Use hunger as your guide."

$\mathcal{L}$ISA LOEB may be best known for "Stay (I Missed You)"—her debut single on the soundtrack of the movie *Reality Bites*—but one of her most significant accomplishments is less obvious. Raised in Dallas, where she says she was highly rewarded for following the rules, she nevertheless imagined and then created an unconventional life for herself as a professional musician. "I felt really frustrated because in my world, creativity wasn't highly valued. Dallas in the 1980s was a very conservative city," she says.

Lisa was an achiever at The Hockaday School, the private school she attended. She was enrolled in many advanced placement classes and was president of the student council. But in addition, she danced in a troupe, acted in an independent movie, was a DJ for three years, wrote and performed songs, and was a program director at an FM radio station based at St. Marks School of Texas.

Though her parents gave her music, dance, and voice lessons, they weren't wild about her choice to become a professional musician out of college. The irony of her parents' resistance is that Lisa, more than most musicians, has managed to establish a sense of safety in her life in order to explore as a performer. Before graduating from Brown University, where she and her singing partner, Elizabeth Mitchell, performed as Liz and Lisa, Lisa was already laying the groundwork for a musical career. She and Liz found a manager. They knew where they were going to live in New York City. And a record company had already expressed interest in their music.

"My concept is that you have to follow your heart to be creative. But it's also really important to create some security so that you have the freedom to be creative," she explains.

Her parents' concerns about developing a secure backup profession were persuasive enough that Lisa did complete one year of a master's program in psychology at New York University. But she discontinued her studies there in order to focus primarily on music. Since that time, she has come out with five CDs: *Tails* (1995), Grammy-nominated *Firecracker* (1997), *Cake and Pie* (2002), *Hello Lisa* (2002), and *The Way It Really Is* (2004).

Following an eclectic muse, she also partnered with Liz on a children's CD and board book called *Catch the Moon* and starred in *#1 Single*, a short series on E!. If you're a foodie, you might have seen her in Food Network's *Dweezil and Lisa*, which she and Dweezil created, produced, and starred in.

Now forty, Lisa is writing to herself at nineteen, while she was still at Brown.

*

Dear Lisa,
Here are seven things you should know that will
make your life a lot easier.

1. You're driven and want to do *every*thing—school,
   extracurricular, and social. But you really don't
   have to work every second of every day.
2. Don't be one of those people who look back and
   say, "I wish I had tried to do that thing I really
   loved." It's good that you're trying out the
   careers that you're interested in. Good for you.
3. There's not only one right way to do things.
4. You've been highly rewarded for following the
   rules. Not following them will feel strange, but
   it will be good for you.
5. Some artists can live hand-to-mouth, but *you*
   need an income to be able to focus on your
   music. That doesn't mean you're not an artist.
6. Don't mistake being an independent-minded
   person with doing it alone. You don't have to
   do it all yourself. You're in charge of creating
   the perfect team and support system for you.
7. Use hunger as your guide. What do you hunger
   to do, that's valuable to you, in and of itself?
   Pay attention to that.

Lisa

· * ·

MEGAN McCAFFERTY

Author

"Be brave now, Meg.
Go ahead and say, 'Hey.'"

*T*HERE IS a simple, supremely comforting antidote to the unbearable self-consciousness, brutally exclusive cliques, unrequited crushes, and rigid social systems of middle and high school: a best friend—the girl with whom you can snort-laugh, talk to 24/7, and face any humiliation. She is all you *really* need to get through those years, but for Megan McCafferty, author of the best-selling novels *Sloppy Firsts, Second Helpings, Charmed Thirds*, and *Fourth Comings,* this girl, Tonya, made only a brief appearance. They became friends, soon to be best friends known as "the Gypsy Twins," at the end of seventh grade, and Tonya moved away two years later.

Megan, who grew up in Bayville, New Jersey, had felt isolated before Tonya's friendship, but after Tonya left it was far worse. "I remember feeling very alone. I didn't feel like there was anybody I could trust, no one really understood me. In order to survive socially, I felt I had to do something that wasn't me," she said, referring to a choice she describes in her letter below.

Today thirty-five-year-old Megan is married and the mother of a five-year-old boy but still looks like the lean runner that both she and her main character, Jessica Darling, were in high school. Jessica's adventures received special attention in 2006 when readers spotted passages in *How Opal Mehta Got Kissed, Got Wild, and Got a Life*, a high-profile first novel by Harvard student Kaavya Viswanathan, that seemed to be closely modeled after sections in Megan's first two books. "It's my hope that I'm remembered for my work as a writer, and that my reluctant role in the controversy is forgotten altogether," she said.

Wearing a wide, black headband, Megan showed me around her recently expanded, neat-as-a-pin house in Princeton, New Jersey, and shared homemade orange, cranberry, and blueberry muffins while we talked about the last three years of high school. She has big, expressive eyes and a ready laugh for the girl she was, who walked around blaming everything and everybody but herself for her bad moods. "If I could go back and tell myself something, it would be don't lie to yourself in thought or in action. Those years I spent not being true to myself, I was very unhappy," she recalled.

Hey Meg-O-My-Leg-O,

That greeting makes no sense. It never did, not even when Tonya first addressed a letter to you in that manner. Her other nicknames for you—My Long-Lost Gypsy Twin, Soul Sista No. 1, The Future Mrs. River Phoenix—are easily interpretable, even twenty years after she originally coined them. But the unabashed absurdity of Meg-O-My-Leg-O hints at the sad truth you know only too well right now, in these first hours after Tonya and her family have moved three hours away:

You will never have another best friend like her.

You can barely resist the urge to hurl a blunt, heavy object across the room. Please drop your algebra textbook and hear me out.

Look, I know you're devastated. I promise I won't be one of those know-it-all adults making light of your anguish. True, you are moping in the sighing, crying, dying way that only a freshgirl in high school can, but this is definitely not a minor setback that you've blown oh-so melodramatically out of proportion. Tonya moving away is not a tip-of-the-nose zit on school picture day. Tonya moving away is not a dirty look from the bitch in your gym class. Tonya moving away is not waiting until a Limited sweater goes on clearance before your mom will buy it for you. Tonya moving away is indeed the major life-changing event you believe it is. It's the defining point of your high school years.

The other girls at Central Regional High School are too superficial or too uptight. Too dorky or too popular. Too quiet when they talk or too noisy when they chew. Too body-obsessed, too boy-obsessed, too Benetton-obsessed. Too any unlikely combination of the aforementioned (and unmentioned) character traits. In short, these other girls are not Tonya. They annoy you endlessly, and you cannot possibly imagine being best friends with any of them. You fear, weekend after weekend, of either staying home alone or going out with these girls and hating every minute of it.

Here's the thing you need to know, Meg-O-My-Leg-O: You have options. I know it doesn't feel like you have options, but you do. You're already too focused on taking the easiest, most socially acceptable option: Saying yes to B., your closest male friend, the future captain of the varsity football and baseball teams who has made it very clear that he wants you to be his girlfriend. You do not have to say yes to B. You do not have to accept B.'s offer of boyfriendship just because you're afraid of being alone.

I know what you're thinking. That within Central Regional High School's complicated caste system you could do far worse than being known as the girlfriend of the future captain of the varsity football and baseball teams. I mean, what could be wrong with being the girlfriend of the future captain of the varsity football and baseball teams? What newly best-friendless girl who hates everyone else at her school would say no to that?

You should say no to that.

B. is not a bad guy. He means well. But B. is not the right guy for you. In fact, his steadfast determination to make you his girlfriend is baffling and inexplicable. Sure, it makes some sense on the surface: two high-achieving, scholar-athletes who will go on to be voted Most Likely to Succeed. But there are serious incompatibles here. For example, B. does not think you're funny. In three and a half years of on-and-off dating, B. will laugh at exactly one of your jokes, and then only because it involves the word "tit." B. also won't understand why you'll want to spend five weeks during the summer before junior year taking vocal music and creative writing classes at Rutgers University with a "bunch of art fags." B. does not appreciate 10,000 Maniacs or Morrissey, *The Bell Jar* or *Life in Hell*, *The Brady Bunch* or *The Breakfast Club*. Now do you see my point?

Say no to B. Stay friends if you can, but that might not be possible for a long time. And don't concern yourself with whomever he chooses to date in order to get over you. She's bound to be a better match for him than you are, and will certainly get more out of wearing his varsity jacket than you ever will. You'll all be better off, believe me.

You want answers. You want to hear about the other options I referred to earlier. You hope to discover that Central Regional High School has its own chapter of S.U.C.K.L.E.S.S. (The Society of Underground Cool Kids Lobbying for the Elimination of Suckage in School) and that I'm here to give you the password for entry.

Well, there is no secret society, but I will give you some choice words of advice: Open up, Meg. Open up your eyes, your mind, your heart to the options; otherwise you are destined to spend the next three and a half years in a pissy mood that is only occasionally interrupted by a somewhat less pissy mood. Where are these options? Everywhere. Everyone around you is an option. Everyone you sit next to in class, pass in the halls, or watch silently from afar is an option. I know that's hard for you to believe because you are perceived as a certain girl at Central Regional High School, a certain girl who is expected to do certain things with certain people. You are the girl who gets straight As. You're the girl who runs cross-country and sings your way into first place in the school talent show. You're the girl who eats lunch at the Honors Table with other smart kids who never get in trouble. Of course, no one knows that you have to bust your ass to get As in math, would rather be playing field hockey, and wish you could be fronting a band instead of singing corny Broadway ballads. No one knows how often you wonder what would happen if you decided to set down your lunch tray with the cheerleaders, the hicks, the stoners.

Actually, one person knows these things about you. But she's not around anymore. And you can't keep punishing others—and in turn, yourself—just because they aren't her.

PLEASE PUT THE ALGEBRA BOOK DOWN.

Each and every person at your school is stifled by their own particular set of expectations. And I guarantee you, Meg, that they are as unhappy with those limits as you are. They, too, wonder what it would be like to upend the social order, to break into off-limits cliques and claim forbidden friendships of their own. They, too, wonder why they can't work up the courage to launch this high school revolution by unleashing a radical, rallying cry, something along the lines of, "Hey. What's up?"

Please don't wait until your senior year to break free and rebel. Be brave now, Meg. Go ahead and say, "Hey." Give others an opportunity to meet the true you, flaws and all, as you've let only Tonya see you. No one can be what she was to you, but there are others who can—and will—offer friendships that are altogether different and satisfying. Appreciate these people for who they are, and don't condemn them for who they are not. Central Regional High School will never be a perfect place, but there are people, ones you overlook every single day, who can make it a hell of a lot more pleasant for the next three and a half years if you let them.

It's true that your most enduring friendships will come after high school graduation. But before you leave Central

Regional High School behind, you will forge a bond that runs far deeper than all others, even your Gypsy Twinship with Tonya. You'll open up to this new best friend when you least expect it, in the second half of your final year of high school. He'll be two years younger than you, and no one will understand the attraction.

Be nice to this boy, Meg, because one day he will be your husband.

Older and wiser,
M.

* ✳ *

Danica McKellar
Actress/Math Whiz/Author

"Just because your feelings are strong, they don't have to make you feel desperate."

AT FIFTEEN, Danica McKellar spent hours staring at herself in the full-length mirror on the back of her bedroom door. Not because she was admiring herself, but because she wondered what was *wrong* with her. Mind you, she was known to millions as the ultimate dream girl Winnie Cooper from *The Wonder Years* . . . so why did she feel so bad?

"At the ages of fourteen, fifteen, and sixteen, I got really obsessed with needing particular guys to like me," remembers Danica. "If they didn't, I thought something was really wrong with me. I'd stare in the mirror, try on make up and different hairstyles, wishing I could find that key thing to make that guy call me back."

You'd think that someone on a TV series, particularly a character viewed as America's sweetheart, wouldn't suffer such anxieties. But "that just shows you how strong female insecurities are at that age and how crucial a time it is in terms of self-awareness," says Danica.

She is now a champion of girls at those vulnerable ages. In particular, she's on a quest to help middle school girls shed their fears in mathematics and build more self-confidence.

Her best-selling 2007 book, *Math Doesn't Suck: How to Survive Middle-School Math Without Losing Your Mind or Breaking a Nail* is like a *Seventeen* magazine version of math. Stuffed with quizzes, horoscopes, girlie details, and word problems featuring real middle school quandaries, the book is a rare example of a boldface name leveraging her celebrity to give girls a positive role model. She shows them: "You can do math!" and "Smart is sexy!"

Of course, not every TV star doubles as a math whiz. Danica graduated summa cum laude as a math major in 1998 from UCLA. While at college, she coauthored a paper that proves a theorem in mathematical physics (now called the "Chayes-McKellar-Winn Theorem.") She's spoken in front of Congress on the importance of women in mathematics, and her mathematics work covered the front page of the *New York Times*' science section on July 19, 2005.

Exemplifying the marriage of math brains with girlie-ness that she depicts in her book, Danica has also provided the voice for sexy Sapphire Stagg on Cartoon Network's *Justice League* and continued to act in roles on *The West Wing*, *How I Met Your Mother*, and in a Lifetime movie, *Inspector Mom*, among others. She's also writing a sequel to the national best seller *Math Doesn't Suck*, which will be called *Kiss My Math* and hits the shelves in July 2008. Its target audience: girls twelve to fifteen.

For her letter, Danica, thirty-three, picked a time during her bedroom-mirror-self-scrutiny phase at fifteen. She met The Guy while on a ski trip arranged as part of a charitable fundraiser. He was the only other child actor among the celebrities, so they spent the entire weekend together. Danica remembers ruefully: "I was absolutely head-over-heels. I thought 'This is the guy!'" Then she got home and waited for him to call. And waited.

*

Dear Danica,

He's not calling, is he?

It's okay, relax. Your life does not depend on that phone ringing or not. I know it feels like the end of the world, but it's not.

"But *why* hasn't he called?" you ask. He might be distracted, he might have a girlfriend already, or any other of a million reasons. But it's not your job to try to figure out which one it is. You'd just be blindly guessing, and more to the point: It *doesn't matter* why he's not calling you. It's not your fault. You are a smart, attractive, talented young woman, and someday you're going to look back on this moment and laugh about how obsessive you were. Seriously. Let it go!

I know, I know. You're currently combing through every detail of the trip, looking for clues as to what his intentions might have been. He taught you a magic trick, you laughed, you talked about how much fun it was and how you'd have to do it again. Didn't that mean anything? I know, you've been trying to answer that same question yourself. For days.

You've talked to your best friend for hours at a time, reliving the trip, and you've both pretty much determined that he should be calling. Didn't he say he would? I mean, why else would you exchange phone numbers? And he's cute and nice and smart and good at magic, and I bet our kids would be adorable, and oh, wouldn't he be just the perfect boyfriend?

So . . . when he never called, you decided to write to him—not an email, but a real live letter, in your handwriting. And when he didn't write you back, you decided, tonight, to call him. The call was weird. He sounded slow. Unenthusiastic. And you, somehow, are deciding that it's *your* fault.

You're replaying the conversation in your mind, wondering what you did wrong—what you should have said, what you shouldn't have said. You've dug out the photocopy of your letter (yes, you made a copy before you sent it) and you're analyzing it more closely than any of your scripts. *Was I too forward? Not forward enough?*

We both know what happened next. Instead of taking the bad phone call as a sign that a relationship wasn't meant to be, you decided: *If I learn some magic, he'll be impressed, and then he'll really be interested in me.* You're going to buy videos and books about magic. You're going to spend months learning how to juggle, tirelessly practicing for someday when you'd be able to show him (which is not going to happen). Your heart is going to be sore for months, especially when you see articles in all the teen magazines about how great he is.

Danica, wake up!!! I want to tell you that it truly doesn't matter if that guy calls you or not. It's not worth the agonizing. You're investing all your hopes and dreams on a kind of person—species Teenage Boy—whose mindset is so utterly different from yours. They've got testosterone rushing through their veins. They're distracted. Girls your age are very focused by comparison.

This may help: Think of yourself as being in development. You go to the gym to exercise. This is the gym for boy-girl relationships. You're gaining experience. You're in training to become the young, fabulous woman and complete person that you will be someday. Don't think of this as a "failed" attempt at a relationship, but rather, as a successful training ground of experience for your future.

You'll learn that just because your feelings are strong, they don't have to make you feel desperate. You'll learn that when you fall for a guy that quickly, what you're really doing is falling for a "fantasy guy" and then putting some new guy's face on it. How could you know someone well enough after one ski trip to decide he was "the one"? Doesn't it seem more reasonable that perhaps you're just looking to fulfill your dream of a fantasy guy? And if you'd met just about *any* other cute, nice guy that weekend, he would have filled the "fantasy guy" job just as well, and you'd be now pining after *him*, instead?

I know all this theory is well and good and that for now, these crushes can still feel pretty painful. Just make sure that the pain you're feeling is only about the loss of a candidate for "fantasy guy"—and not about what you think is lacking in *you*.

Love yourself when you look in that mirror, and when the right guy comes along, I promise he'll love you, too— and for all the right reasons.

With so much love and understanding,
Danica

· ✳ ·

Tara McPherson

Artist

*"It's every child's birthright to be loved and
cared for—including yours."*

Tara McPherson was wearing pigtails, serious eyeliner, and her shoulder-to-wrist tattoos when we met in her
Brooklyn studio. At thirty-one she has already had a prolific
and profitable artist's career, fostered by an impressive work
ethic. She sleeps late, gets to the studio at noon or one o'clock,
and happily works till midnight before meeting friends for
drinks or dinner.

Her comics and covers have appeared regularly in DC Ver-
tigo publications. She has illustrated for companies such as
Pepsi and *Spin* magazine. And she is well known as a poster
artist for rock bands. A recent Beck poster won *Esquire*'s
award for Best Poster of 2006. Oh, yes, she also designs toys
for Kidrobot, teaches, and plays bass in a band.

Tara graduated from art school with a five-year plan, but
her success is more attributable to events that took place in her
teens than a career strategy. Embroiled in alcohol and drug
problems, her parents fought verbally and physically when she
was growing up. They finally decided to divorce when she was
thirteen. "My home life sucked, but I was always really strong

and resilient to it. So when they decided to divorce, it was a really good thing," says Tara.

A couple of months before they split, Tara began having strange aches and pains. Then her mother broke some shocking news. The man who Tara had always assumed was her father, whom her mother was now divorcing, was not. She was actually the product of a sperm donor, whom her mother had sought out during a previous marriage when she had trouble getting pregnant.

"It was very traumatic—like losing your identity," Tara recalls. Shortly after, she consulted a neurologist about her mysterious pains. He diagnosed syringomyelia, a fluid-filled cyst. It was caused by an undetected condition called Chiari Malformation, where the bottom part of Tara's brain was descending out of the skull and crowding her spinal cord.

Normally, the disorder is monitored for years before doctors recommend surgery. But the turmoil in her life, Tara believes, accelerated the process. Within three weeks of detecting the cyst, her vision was blurring, and she couldn't walk. So she had an eight-hour surgical decompression procedure, which involved cutting off the bottom part of her skull and part of her cervical vertebrae, and had a skin graft sewn into the dura to allow more room for the spinal fluid to flow properly.

The drama continued. Tara remembers her parents fighting and yelling in the intensive care unit just after the operation. But the operation and her subsequent life with her mother had a long-reaching effect. "I think my survival instincts really kicked in. I thought, 'I'm here. I'm alive. I want to be all I can be,'" she remembers. "I've always been extremely independent. But I began to realize that, like, the only person who is going to take care of me is me."

Her mother didn't work, so they lived on welfare and food stamps in Playa Del Rey, California. Tara visted her father in nearby Westchester occasionally and worked as a hostess at a pizza parlor, one of many jobs she would have throughout high school and college. Now thirty-one and working on a graphic novel, Tara is writing to herself at fourteen, about a year after her parents' divorce when her mom was almost never home.

Tara,

You don't even know how much you need a parent. That's how strong you are. You'd rather not have your mom around because she's always wasted. So when she takes off with a guy she meets in a bar, which she does all the time, you love it. You go to school, go to your job, feed yourself, meet your friends. It's easier that way.

Your mom's idea of parenting? She knows you love Twix candy bars. So when she's headed out she'll say, "Tara, I'm going down to the liquor store. I'll get you a Twix."

"Sure, whatever," you answer.

She leaves, disappears with a random guy for three days, and when she comes back home she says, "Look, Tara, here's your Twix." Like it makes everything okay.

You laugh about this. That's how strong you are. But you hate her. There is a world of hurt in that hate. A world that you will plumb in your art. Your signature style is adorable, innocent faces and creatures who leak pathos or menace.

Sometimes I Just Want A Hug is a painting of a beautiful girl with perfect, bluish-teal hair, heavy eyeliner, an upturned nose, and a giant heart-shaped hole in her chest. The heart-shaped hole features candy-cane-striped bars running from top to bottom, one of which is broken.

Love's Lost Lust, a silkscreen, shows another beautiful girl who is blonde, pony-tailed, naked with pert breasts, and a tattoo of a dagger dripping blood on her arm.

You are raising yourself and doing it amazingly well. Your older sister ran away. Your younger brother will develop a crystal meth addiction. It will take them years before they turn around their lives . . . but eventually they will. Unlike them you will make it out of your so-called childhood alive and healthy, and you'll succeed as an artist.

But . . . what can I tell you? As an adult you will be too strong sometimes. Your boyfriends will call you an ice princess. Other times, they'll say you're too needy. If you could, somehow, I wish you'd find yourself an adult who will give you some of what you need. Your aunt. A teacher. You need to be able to lean on *someone*, if only to know that it can be done. It's every child's birthright to be loved and cared for—including yours.

It sounds too embarrassing to ask for anything, especially when you know you can do everything on your own. But think of this: Sometimes asking for help from someone who can give it, is a gift to them, not an imposition.

Still strong,
Tara McPherson, Lonely Heart

* ✳ *

AIMEE MULLINS

Paralympic Athlete/Model/Actress

*"The more you try to tame
the wild thing that you are,
the less wonderful your life will be."*

I DIDN'T know what to expect when I met Aimee Mullins for lunch at Gemma, a bistro next to the Bowery Hotel in Manhattan. A yard-long list of accomplishments provided by her publicist included a predictably humbling array of feats (world record-holder athlete, president of the Women's Sports Foundation) for a thirty-two-year-old. But it also displayed a remarkable range. Olympian athlete *and* runway model? Division I track competitor *and* actress? One of three students selected for a full academic scholarship from the U.S. Department of Defense . . . *and* named to *Rolling Stone*'s annual "Hot List"?

Oh yeah, and all of this on silicone and titanium prosthetic legs. Aimee was born with fibular hemimelia, a condition in which the shin bones are partially or totally absent. Her parents decided to have both of her legs amputated below the knee when she was one year old, with the hope that she would be able to walk rather than use a wheelchair for the rest of her life.

The model part of her lengthy resume became instantly understandable when she walked toward our table. Tall and slender, she has long, sandy blonde hair and wideset hazel eyes that radiate candor. Wearing a peasant-style blouse, she looks like the girl next door whom everyone has a crush on. A quick perusal of Google Images shows how far up those natural good looks can be ratcheted. She morphs from fashion queen to intergalactic android to glossy celebrity. One arresting black-and-white photo, by Lynn Johnson, of her wearing her cheetah-styled sprinting prostheses is part of a permanent exhibit of the "Greatest American Women of the 20th Century" at the Women's Museum in Dallas.

Aimee was still mourning the loss of her cat, Socks, a twenty-year-old "superstar" who never seemed to age until her sudden demise a week earlier. "She has been with me since my childhood, so I'm feeling strangely orphaned now," she told me.

Growing up with two brothers in Allentown, Pennsylvania, Aimee played softball, volleyball, soccer, and raced on skis. She attended Georgetown University on that Defense Department scholarship and entered her first meet for disabled racers one summer when she was bored by her job at the Pentagon. "Initially, I just wanted to get out of work for a couple days," she says. "I had always competed against people with legs. I didn't know anything. I went to this meet with wooden legs. I was like some girl under a rock with 1930's technology—but I won running against people with high-tech legs."

What can I do next? she wondered. She signed up for the long jump. A guy at the meet came up to her and said, "I hear you're a double BK."

"I didn't know the lingo. I thought, 'What's that—a hamburger?'" laughs Aimee. It stands for double below-the-knee amputee. He told Aimee that she wasn't supposed to be able to do the long jump. That's when she looked at the eight guys who had entered the event. Sure enough. They each had one good leg.

No matter. Aimee came within four inches of the national record that day, and within a year she owned the world record. She's still the only double BK to attempt it.

The rest of the athletic story is just as amazing. She joined Georgetown's women's track team, the first disabled member to compete on an NCAA track team in history. She then trained, qualified for, and competed in the Paralympics in Atlanta in 1996 only eighteen months later. In addition to the long jump, she set world records there for the one hundred-and two hundred-meter sprints.

She has since collected a broad portfolio of accolades and accomplishments as a speaker, board member, fashion model, athlete, and actress. In 2006 she appeared in Siofra Campbell's *Marvelous,* Oliver Stone's *World Trade Center*, and Carlos Brooks's *Quid Pro Quo.* With such roles—and future ones that she hopes will come her way—another limitation associated with being "disabled" falls thunderously to the ground. This one has personal reverberations. When Aimee announced her intention to become an actress after playing the lead in a school play, her aunt said, "You'll never make it. Hollywood only wants perfect people."

Aimee, thirty-two, writes to herself at twenty-one, after the 1996 Paralympics Games in Atlanta.

*

Dear Aimee,

You're almost through college, and you're ready for "real life." But try not to grow up too much. Always notice the magic in everyday life. The more "realistic" you become, the more control and planning you try to exert over your life—the more you try to tame the wild thing that you are—the less wonderful your life will be.

Surprised? I know. The message every older person seems to want to send to a younger person is: Be focused, responsible; plan your life and then work hard because that leads to success and maturity. But adulthood is not about being inflexible and unafraid. You must not try to prevent the happy accidents that are strewn throughout life. Being "responsible" is really about being a consciously present, self-accountable adult.

From twelve to twenty you've been a super achiever— trying to become organized and sensible, invulnerable to the prospect of failure. You ran your paper route, cleaned the house, and made the dinners at home. College was a solo project. You had to scare up a ride to the SATs and find your own way to the Defense Department scholarship. Oh, Aim, I now know that you could have gone to *any* college in the country for free . . . but who in your world back in Allentown knew enough to tell you that?

Okay, so training yourself to become disciplined and serious has paid off beyond belief in some ways. You're an Olympic athlete, and you've learned the incredible power of determination. But . . . here's the big But: Being a super achiever isn't about developing the habits of someone who is rigid, impervious, and unrelenting to any idea of "failure" or "weakness." That isn't real strength, and it isn't the best place for you.

You're a dreamer, and yet daydreaming is something you've forgotten how to do. I want you to relearn how to be naïve. Being naïve isn't about being unaware, it's about being curious. It's a different way of having an ongoing conversation with yourself about possibilities, about the potential both within and around you. Your naïveté made you fearless. It was as much a part of your successes as being responsible and determined.

In society you're encouraged to drop naïveté. You're encouraged to be realistic. But what is being realistic for a girl without two ordinary legs? Being realistic would mean that you would have never learned how to walk on prosthetic legs. Or that it would take months to learn, instead of the days it took you. Or that you'd never have even tried the long jump, let along four-inch stilettos on a runway alongside supermodels, which you'll do soon.

You were right to always resist this yoke of being "disabled." Growing up, you were expected to do anything and everything as well as or better than others. Making high honors. Playing musical instruments. Winning local art contests. Skiing. Sports of all kinds—against *able-bodied* kids because that's who your brothers, cousins, and friends were. Only you decided your limits because if you could imagine it, you believed you could do it. Your report cards always had As for grades and minuses for attitude. "Aimee is never really 'with' us," the teachers would write. Of *course* you weren't. You were in ancient Egypt. Or sailing on the high seas. Jousting for a seat at the Round Table!

There's a lot to be said for a belief in yourself and your ability that comes from that childlike place, from a trusting mind of a six-year-old. Einstein said: "The gift of fantasy has meant more to me than my talent for absorbing positive knowledge." People will always be commenting on your determination, but you must remember the key role your curiosity played in shaping who you are and who you will become.

A decade from now you'll find it immensely powerful to be around a group of six-year-olds. You'll walk into a classroom of kids whose parents have carefully prepared them to meet a woman without legs—a *disabled* woman. But then you tell them about the cheetah-legs that made you the fastest woman in the world on prostheses. When you ask them which animal's or superhero's or cartoon character's legs they'd want if they wanted to be able to jump over a roof or make a fast escape, they immediately scream *a kangaroo! No, a frog! No, Go-Go Gadget!* And just like you did, they don't see deficiency when they see your legs; they see pure potential. To these kids you're not disabled—you're super-abled.

Surround yourself with the fantastical. You have everything you need inside of you already. You don't have to see the whole journey laid out in front of you so you can "plan" for it. Honor the magic; be present for the adventure. Just trust that if you get from A to B, the next step C (or whatever letter you jump to!) will reveal itself. Keep the dreamer alive. It's who you really are.

Love,
Me

· ✳ ·

Mary Osborne
Professional Surfer

"You are afraid to take the path that is
calling to you."

$\mathcal{B}$ECAUSE Mary Osborne was raised on Solimar Beach in Ventura, California, with three older brothers who surfed, it was the most natural thing in the world for her to pick up a surfboard. But she probably never would have become the winner of MTV's 2003 Surf Girls reality show, in which fourteen girls competed for a wildcard entry into the World Championship Tour of Surfing Pro Contest, if she hadn't been so short. Only five feet four inches, she was in high school when she began to realize that her height was limiting her in basketball and volleyball. That's when surfing began to take on new meaning.

"Those years are when I discovered surfing as an outlet. Instead of being involved in group sports during that crucial time, I kind of went on my own individual route. I could work my aggressions out in an activity that was a separate thing, away from family," remembers Mary.

A longboarder (using boards nine feet and longer), she continued to improve and at age sixteen had begun making a name for herself in surfing magazines and competitions. By the time she was ready to graduate from high school, she found herself wishing she could surf full-time. "I applied everywhere possible, hoping I wouldn't get in. When the responses came back, I was more pleased by the denials than the acceptances," she says.

But college was clearly what her family expected for her. She went to Santa Barbara City College for two years, feeling more and more that she was in the wrong place. Her parents—a teacher and a dentist—were firm about Mary continuing college—just as her three brothers had. They couldn't understand how a surfer, much less a female longboarder, could make a living.

After two years, Mary transferred to the University of California at Santa Barbara and during her first semester there, all her feelings came to a head. She remembers walking back to her car on Thursdays, her longest day of classes, and breaking down in tears because her life felt so wrong. After seeing how unhappy she was, her parents finally agreed to let her take a few months off to sort it all out.

Within a week of that decision, she got a phone call inviting her to be part of MTV's Surf Girls competition. She couldn't have asked for a more concrete sign. Filming started immediately in Australia, Samoa, Tahiti, and Hawaii. After winning the MTV contest, Mary became a professional surfer, on both shortboards and longboards. She has coauthored a book, *Sister Surfer: A Woman's Guide to Surfing with Bliss and Courage,* and is sponsored by Patagonia, Etnies Shoes, Angel Eyewear, Robert August Surfboards, wet n wild Cosmetics, and others. Mary is writing to herself at twenty, when she was still wrestling with what she should do about college and surfing.

*

Dear Mary,

There's something you've never tried to describe to anyone about surfing. Waiting, on the water, falling and rising with the horizon. The feel of the sun. The water running its soft tongue over you. How you merge with all that, how you are able to insert yourself into the crook of a wave like you belong. Because you do belong. You're a competitor and you love attacking, but ever since your teenage years surfing has also been your backyard, therapist, and playtime all rolled into one.

You are afraid to take the path that is calling to you. How will you make money as a surfer? How will you grow into a well-rounded, educated person? Your parents see college as the essential next step. But you feel that you've already been getting the education you truly care about as you travel up and down the state for competitions, meeting interesting people, and managing your fledgling career.

Your family's example is so powerful that it's hard to resist. All three of your brothers are talented, beautiful surfers. But they went to college and are pursuing "real" careers. To reject a college diploma is to reject one of your family's core values.

It's more than that, though. Choosing surfing as your main focus is also the problem. Your mom was the only girl in her family and had seven brothers. Then she got married and had three sons and one daughter. She's super feminine, in part, because she's always been surrounded by males. "Remember, you're a lady," she always says.

So choosing surfing is like rejecting your mom's hopes for that lady she wanted you to turn into. But honestly, Mary, your mom wants what's best for you. Now is the time for *you* to decide what that is. And besides . . . who says ladies don't surf??!

Your sister surfer,
Mary

. ✳ .

SABINA LOUISE PIERCE

Photographer

"What doesn't kill you
will make you stronger."

THE MAGIC of inspiration is how it leaps, for no discern-
able reason, from a person, a story, or an object into your soul
and takes up lodging there. For Sabina Louise Pierce, inspiration came in the form of a big bay thoroughbred with a band-
aged right hind leg, lying on a raft device in a swimming pool.
It was Barbaro, the Kentucky Derby winner who broke his
ankle while racing in the Preakness Stakes, after a five-hour
operation on May 21, 2006, at University of Pennsylvania's
New Bolton Center in Kennett Square, Pennsylvania.

Sabina, a freelance photographer who works for the *New
York Times* and *The Christian Science Monitor,* among other
papers, had been called by UPenn's New Bolton Center
to document Barbaro's post-surgery moments. A horse- and
animal-lover, she became the only photographer allowed to
shoot the beloved racehorse from that time on. "To watch this
big, beautiful horse in that pool was mesmerizing," Sabina
remembers. "There was a nurse sitting there on this walkway
they put across the pool. She was stroking his hair and whis-
pering in his ear. I wanted to crawl out there and touch him.

When he started to wake up and they pulled him up in the air, I knew that was the shot."

The next day almost every major newspaper, news Web site, and news show in the country featured Sabina's photograph of the giant equine, a blue blindfold over his eyes, dangling over the swimming pool. Her reaction, she says, "was funny. I wasn't thinking 'This is my photograph.' To me it was: 'The whole nation cares about this horse.'"

Of course, Sabina had known who Barbaro was prior to that meeting. She felt his charisma, even from afar, and says you could tell he knew he was a rock star. Later, her understanding grew more nuanced. "Once I got to know him and got really close, I just wanted to hang out with him. He reminds me of the Dalai Lama. He has a young heart and an old soul," she told me as we sat outdoors eating lunch at the White Dog Café in Philadelphia where she lives. Maddie, the eight-year-old fox terrier who accompanies Sabina almost everywhere, sat patiently beside our table, her portable water bowl next to her feet.

Sabina's relationship with Barbaro deepened in an unexpected way in October of 2006. Sabina was cantering on her horse, Toby, in a race when the horse was spooked and jumped sideways. Sabina's body flipped off. She landed on her back and fractured her T-12 vertebrae. After a CAT scan at a local hospital, doctors found her spinal cord was so compressed that they thought she would be paralyzed. Then began a medical journey that Sabina sees as parallel to Barbaro's.

"They medevaced me to the University of Pennsylvania, just like Barbaro. I had surgery the next day, where they put in rods and screws, just like Barbaro. They fused my spine. They fused his leg. We both had amazing surgeons. We both had miracles—him because his bone didn't come through his leg and me because I did not become paralyzed," she explains. She believes his inspiration helped her heal much more quickly than her surgeon expected.

During her three months of recovery, when she was not allowed to be near Barbaro because it would be too dangerous, she began work on a book called *For the Love of Barbaro*. It chronicles his relationship with the caretakers who had become his family and the avalanche of emotion that rolled toward him during his last eight months of life. In her letter, Sabina is writing to herself at fourteen, when her role in the life of such a great and influential animal was unimaginable.

Dear Sabina,

You've gotten used to being a loner. Kids pick on you at school. Someone calls you fat. Someone else in the hall makes fun of you for being a jock and everyone laughs. You try to make your face expressionless, like you didn't notice (riiight) or don't care (yeah, sure), but it feels like you will never get through those moments. Everything slows way down. You can feel every flaw in your body and face and hair grow bigger as the eyes turn toward you. You and your collection of horrors make your way through the hallway like you're moving through syrup.

You want to be accepted, Sabina. You want it so badly that you just deprived yourself of one of the most important things in your life. The boy you have a crush on came to school one day and said you smelled like a horse.

So, just like that, you gave up horses.

Sabina, the smell of horses and dogs is one of the most supremely comforting smells in the world to you. Hanging out with animals brings you peace. It's a measure of how bad things are that you've thrown away that joy and consolation. And I won't lie. Things are going to get worse for a while.

Your father will continue to be psychologically cruel, cornering you during the court-ordered holidays you're required to spend with him. He knows how to reduce you and your sisters to quivering messes. You'll also be wounded regularly in your fights with your sister.

What doesn't kill you will make you stronger. That's your mantra. It gets you through. More important, it is true. You will become very strong. Being a loner is sharpening your observant powers, perfect for the photographer you'll become.

Being a loner will also suit your future life as a freelancer, which is how you will get the opportunity to tell one of the greatest photographic stories ever— a story that unites your love of horses with your craft.

Your muse will appear, and he'll be bigger, more handsome, and more generous than any of the specimens walking in the school hallway.

With love,
Sabina

· ✳ ·

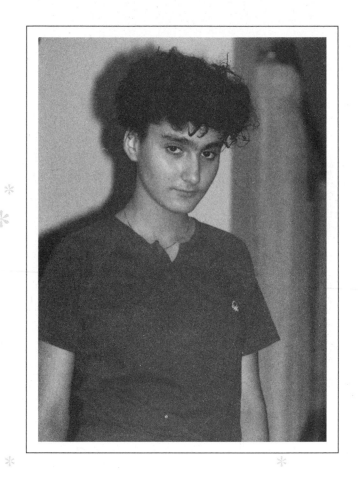

Atoosa Rubenstein

Founder of Alpha Kitty

*"You will find yourself in the future as you
imagine yourself."*

IN SEVENTH grade Atoosa Behnegar entered Valley
Stream North High School, a Long Island public school that
teaches kids from seventh through twelfth grades. It was a
wilderness of *Flashdance* fashion, Italian American culture and
mullet and tail hairstyles. For Atoosa, a Tehran-born immigrant who moved to the United States when she was three, it
was like going from the playground straight into an inferno.

At North, nothing was right about her. Her family didn't
eat the same food and didn't have the same traditions as everyone else. Her mother mortified Atoosa by dressing her in Yves
Saint Laurent clothing that her relatives would send from
Europe and by refusing to let her shave her legs or pluck her
eyebrows. Worse, her grade school friends had all defected to a
different school, leaving her to face the intimidating teenagers
alone.

"When you're in a school with mostly younger children, it
doesn't matter if you're goofy. But once you're in seventh
grade, the twelfth graders might as well be supermodel
women," she said when we met for lunch at Café Luxem-
bourg, a bistro on Manhattan's Upper West Side.

But all of that was mere backdrop for the horrors to come.

A short, muscular, mullet-styled eleventh grader named Nick singled her out almost immediately. He and his friends screamed at her every time they saw her. If they spotted her through a classroom window from a different classroom across a courtyard, they opened the window in order to yell at her. They grabbed every opportunity to shout at her for two years until they graduated. If they screamed actual words, Atoosa has blocked them from her memory.

"It was so scary to me as a young person. It was like I was an animal being hunted. I didn't know why they chose me. It seemed like I was the only one persecuted," she remembers.

Let's hope Nick and his cavemen brethren know what became of the lonely, unibrowed kid they tortured. Now Atoosa Rubenstein (wearing a tiara, she married Ari in 1998), she has alabaster skin that contrasts sharply with her long, inky black hair and eyebrows. Tall, she wears her sophisticated threads, shoes, and purses with casual elegance, fitting for a magazine industry wunderkind who launched her career as a fashion editor. While attending Barnard in 1991, she got her first internship at Lang Communications. Seven years later she founded *CosmoGIRL!* and was named editor in chief—at twenty-six, the youngest editor in chief in Hearst Magazines' one hundred–year history.

After building the new magazine's circulation up to 1.25 million, Atoosa was anointed editor in chief of *Seventeen* in 2003 by Hearst. There she reversed declining newsstand sales with growth of twenty-three percent by 2005.

But this warp speed trajectory left her dissatisfied as she saw her audience gravitate toward the Internet while the magazine industry resorted to ever more desperate measures to hold on to readers. Just as important, she began to recognize her addiction to approval from her bosses. "I was a call girl in the sense that I knew what I needed to do in order to please everybody. In reality I was so unhappy," she says.

So she quit. Her next act was still taking shape when we met. Its key ingredient will be lots of digital contact with girls thirteen to thirty, whom she calls her tribe. Her MySpace page, which has attracted more than thirty-five thousand friends, has become Atoosa's forum for advice-giving and the launch pad for her new company, Big Momma Productions. First out of the hatch is the brand Alpha Kitty, which Atoosa brings to life in a series of videos in partnership with YouTube.

One of the best things Atoosa brings to her tribe, though, has nothing to do with technology. It's her empathy. She really does know how bad it can get as a teenager. At Valley Stream, she used to try out different personas with different sets of people because she felt her real self was so unacceptable.

"I remember this one girl who was known as a bad-ass girl. She had a really long tail, and it was assumed that she did drugs. I sort of became her little friend," she said. Atoosa went as far as buying $5 worth of pills—what kind she wasn't sure—putting on a blasé attitude to suggest she was accustomed to such transactions. Secretly she was terrified of the pills.

With another group of kids, she pretended that her parents were wealthy. "I remember inferring things about myself that were not true. I became a liar—all just trying to find my place," she said, marveling at what she was willing to do to fit in. Here is her letter to herself at thirteen, from the vantage point of being thirty-five.

*

Oh Atoosa,

My heart breaks as I watch you bewildered by these tormentors. You are trying so hard to find a way, *any* way not to be You! But as lost as you are, I'm not going to throw you a pity party because those fantasy scenarios you imagine yourself in? Well . . . one day, they'll come true.

I know you don't believe me, just like you don't believe Mom when she tells you that you are beautiful. *But* I'll say it anyway: One day you will lead a very fancy life. Yes! A girl like you whose parents work multiple jobs and barely make ends meet can grow up to live in a beautiful corner apartment in Manhattan overlooking the water, have weekend houses in the Hamptons and Miami, attend fashion shows in Europe and be photographed for magazines.

And maybe in seventh grade you have no real friends and even fewer romantic prospects, but you *will* find love and a gorgeous, successful husband who's crazy about you. You will say to him, "Had I only known that you would be waiting for me, it would have helped so much."

I know this will happen for you because here I am— here *we* are, because you're always with me—and we're living that life. And even though you think it's impossible, that it could never, ever happen to you, it will . . . and it will happen far earlier in life than you could hope it would. And *you* made it happen. You cope with this lonely, daily life by daydreaming of a better place for yourself. Your fantasies are vivid, they're over-the-top. In them, you're a rock star . . . the kind of person whose autograph everyone wants . . . the kind of person who everyone turns to look at.

And because those fantasies are your only friends, you have this incredible perception of yourself. Thank God for that. Because it will inspire you to keep pushing forward and reaching for the stars . . . and you'll invent a magazine for other girls like you. Thanks to your success with this, *you will find yourself in the future as you imagine yourself.*

I want you to understand the long-term power of a picture in your head. As long as you can see that picture and keep walking toward it, when you're a leader, your troops will follow you to that place. Your troops are the people who work with you. We call them troops because as you've learned, sometimes life can feel like war. Together you will lead your audience to their own better place even when all the signs and haters around them suggest otherwise.

With much love and respect from the better place, *Alpha You*

. ✳ .

Zainab Salbi

Founder of Women for Women International

"Deny the voice inside you, deny your instinct
. . . and you will live a prolonged death."

A LIVELY, dark-haired beauty with a spectacular smile, Zainab Salbi is the founder of Women for Women International, an innovative not-for-profit that supports and nurtures women victims of war. For much of her childhood in Iraq she was called the "the pilot's daughter." This moniker was defining not because pilots were rare, but because her father was the personal pilot for Saddam Hussein.

Being Hussein's pilot was much more than a job for Baba—as Zainab called her father—and his family. Before Hussein appointed Baba to be his pilot, Hussein was an occasional, not particularly welcome part of Zainab's parents' social circle. After his appointment, Zainab's family was required to participate in regular social events, host Hussein during unexpected house calls, and live in a farmhouse near Hussein's country house every weekend. Zainab and her brothers were taught to call him "Amo," the word for uncle.

The relationship was like a noose. Zainab describes the unwritten rules in her memoir (written with Laurie Becklund) *Between Two Worlds, Escape from Tyranny: Growing Up in the Shadow of Saddam.* "When you were with Amo, you were always polite and pleasant. You had no opinions or personal preferences except those that matched his own. There was nothing you'd rather do than spend time with him. . . . If you were a child, you never spoke in his company unless he asked you direct questions, and you always arranged your face to look up at him in adoration."

During Zainab's college years, she encountered the gravest threat possible: Hussein's attraction to her. Zainab was unaware of it, but her mother, Alia, was all too keenly alert. After Zainab broke off an engagement when she was nineteen, Alia perceived that in Hussein's eyes Zainab was a desirable woman, no longer his pretend "niece."

The situation made Zainab's mother feel desperate to protect her daughter. Hussein did whatever he pleased, including routinely using and discarding young women. Alia hatched a plan to get Zainab out of Iraq by arranging a marriage to a thirty-three-year-old Iraqi émigré living in Chicago. Shocking as this plan was to Zainab, who had been raised to be an independent, self-directed woman, she complied because she had lost confidence after her failed engagement.

"I had had a horrible relationship with another guy, and my mother had saved me from it," she told me. "So I wanted to be a good daughter. I thought if I just listen to my mother everything will be fine, even though it went against every aspect of my body and my upbringing."

The marriage, in 1990 when Zainab was twenty, turned ugly immediately. Her husband was cruel in his sexual acts from the first time he touched her on their wedding night—so much so that she could not have sex for a few days. That upset him and made him verbally abusive toward her. He accused her of all kinds of things, from not being womanly to not being a virgin (which was a violation of Zainab's honor, culturally). He gave her an allowance of $20 a week, expected her to press a shirt for him each morning, and insisted that she discontinue her education and get a real estate license instead.

"I cooked, though he ridiculed my painstaking efforts every night at the dinner table, sometimes in front of guests. I felt poor and vulnerable and utterly dependent on him, both financially and emotionally. When I asked him for more money midweek, he made me recite everything I'd spent the first twenty dollars on and criticized me for wasting money on two greeting cards for friends in Iraq," she writes in *Between Two Worlds*. Zainab could not understand why her mother, a lifelong feminist, had pushed her into the marriage.

As bad as it was in the beginning, the abuse got worse. On Zainab's twenty-first birthday, three months after the wedding, her husband raped her, all the while cursing her. Afterward she got in the shower, sobbing. When she got out, he told her to get ready to go out to dinner with his mother. A fight ensued, during which Zainab bit her husband on the arm and he, ridiculously, called 911 to report the domestic violence. Zainab asked the policeman to take her out of the house when she realized that she could not stay with her husband. At the station, she called a friend of her mother's. The next day, while her husband was at work, they returned to Zainab's apartment and packed all her belongings.

All she wanted to do was to return home, but Iraq had invaded Kuwait a month and a half after Zainab had arrived in the United States. The international community had imposed a sanction and an embargo on Iraq, which had closed its borders and triggered cancellation of all international flights and phone service.

Zainab then began the long journey of reinventing herself, on her own. Living with an uncle of her father's in Los Angeles, she worked two retail jobs and in 1991 moved to Washington where she worked and completed her college study at George Mason University. She met and in time began to trust in her love for Amjad Atallah, a recent University of Virginia graduate.

Six months after her marriage to Amjad, Zainab was propelled into her life's work by a *Time* magazine story about rape camps in Bosnia-Herzegovina and Croatia, where women were being held and raped day and night, apparently by Serbian soldiers.

"These weren't informal bivouacs in the forest; the Serbian Army took over hotels and schools and public buildings for this purpose," writes Zainab. "They would release their victims late into pregnancy so they could not abort their 'Serbian' babies, and their families would feel shamed and would abandon them. . . . Rape was every bit as much a strategy of war as the ethnic cleansing fought with guns, perhaps more so because it didn't just eliminate individuals, it destroyed whole families and societies."

In 1993, she and Amjad conceived of an organization that would pair each of these victims of war with another woman—a sponsor, or "sister," who would send a small monthly sum. Named Women for Women International, Zainab's flourishing organization now empowers one hundred twenty thousand survivors of war each year. Sponsors' contributions are channeled into direct aid, rights education, job skills training, and small business development. *Time* magazine named Zainab "Innovator of the Month" in 2005 for her pioneering work as a philanthropist.

As Zainab was building Women for Women, only one bruise remained from her earlier life—her hurt and puzzlement over why her mother had thrust her into a horrible marriage. When Alia, in failing health, came to live with her daughter, Zainab finally learned about the threat Saddam had posed to her. Now thirty-eight, she is writing to herself at twenty, about the bridegroom that her mother was urging upon her.

Dear Zanooba,

I wish you could hear my voice loud and clear as you get off the plane that just landed in Chicago from Iraq. You are about to meet the man who you came here to marry. I know that nothing in him will attract you—or truly convince you of Mama's suggestion that it is a wise thing to accept his marriage proposal.

You'll feel anxious once you look at him and engage in conversation with him. But rather than listening to that anxious feeling in your chest, to the tightness in your throat, or to that whisper in your head that says *This is not making sense*, you will start looking for the small things that you can find in him—some evidence that maybe he will be a nice husband. When that fails, you will lie to yourself fully, ignore your instinct and your feelings, and try to convince yourself that the words he utters are honest and true.

And despite every single instinct, every single feeling, despite even Baba's concerns and your brother's sadness, and despite the million *NOs* in your head, you will go ahead and utter the word *Yes* when he asks you to marry him. Your *Yes* is not for you, not for him, not for your brothers or father, who cried throughout the event. It is simply for Mama. She cries. She refuses to take you back to Iraq. You worry about the societal embarrassment of breaking up a marriage before it takes place. You are giving yourself up to make Mama happy.

So here I am telling you today, please believe that voice inside you. Do not deny your truth. Do not deny your instinct. Say your *NO* as you felt it, as you wanted to say it out loud. You should live your truth. To do that you need to be strong about believing in yourself. Living your truth will not always be easy. There will be times when you may need to go against what societal rules, norms, traditions, and cultures want you to do. It is not easy to go against all of what seems to be so powerful and so unchangeable. But not everything comes easy and free. And to live your truth is also to live in freedom.

You have one life to live; live it fully, and live it freely. Adjusting to the expectations of others will never give you your truth. Enslavement appears in different forms. There is mental bondage, and there is physical bondage. You are lucky not to be physically enslaved. So don't allow anybody to mentally enslave you. That is your responsibility and yours only.

Just as there is one life to live, there is one death to have. Don't allow traditions, cultural expectations, or even what is perceived as the "norm," make you live a prolonged death. Deny the voice inside you, deny your instinct, your sense of right and wrong, your sense of justice, and you will live a prolonged death. But it is not worth it.

I am now thirty-eight. Every time I have denied my truth, I soon realized that it was neither right nor worth it. Fear is sometimes imposed on you, but many times fear is also your own creation. You have a responsibility to nourish it or defeat it. Every time I have nourished my fear, I only prolonged my living death. Every time I fought my fear, I lived my truth and my freedom.

So my twenty-year-old Zainab, you are too young to live a death . . . be strong, be true, be free, and listen to that voice inside you, and say the *NO* that you want to say when he asks you to marry him. Say the *NOs* that you have wanted to say in so many moments in your life. I see that you have prolonged the agony for many years by not saying or living your truth, for allowing yourself to be held hostage by fear.

Live your life, Zainab. . . . Live it fully. . . , Say no to him. Life is too short and too beautiful not to live it fully.

Yours . . .
Zainab

. ✳ .

ARIEL SCHRAG

Comic Book Artist

"Always be sure to be proud of the art you're creating."

$\mathcal{R}$ELENTLESS self-scrutiny is nothing new for middle schoolers and high-school kids. But Ariel Schrag was the rare adolescent who decided to share her story—private fears, crushes, sexual mishaps, drug encounters, and chemistry-grade obsessions included—with *everyone*. Each summer she chronicled the prior school year in a comic book and then photocopied and sold the book at school the following year. Her years at Berkeley High School, in Berkeley, California, where she grew up, are captured in *Awkward, Definition, Potential,* and *Likewise*. In 2008, Touchstone/Simon & Schuster will republish *Awkward, Definition,* and *Potential,* and publish, for the first time, *Likewise*.

Ariel's fearless self-exposure earned her early recognition of the sort that few college kids experience. During her senior year at Columbia University, director Sharon Barnes filmed the documentary *Confession: A Film About Ariel Schrag,* which won the NewFest Audience Award in 2004. And just before graduation in 2003 Killer Films optioned *Potential,* her junior-year story that detailed her parents' divorce and her relationship with her first real girlfriend. After graduating from college, the money from writing the screenplay gave her the chance and the confidence to pursue her artistic interests in New York.

She went through a precarious period after the film money dried up and before she landed a gig as a writer on *The L Word*, a Showtime series featuring lesbian and bisexual characters. Currently living in Los Angeles with her girlfriend, Ariel, twenty-seven, writes to herself at twenty-four, about a year after graduating, during that scrimping and scrounging period in Brooklyn.

*

Ariel,

You planned to make it as an artist when you moved to Brooklyn after graduation.

More like *Definition* anxiety.

The money from the screenplay is almost gone, and your comics still aren't making any money. You and your friend are trying to sell your comics on Bedford St. for, what, $20 a day—$50 if you're lucky. Will you be able to make it as an artist?

Don't waste your time worrying about this, Ariel. You may feel desperate now—trying to piece together enough money with teaching jobs, caricaturing, being a medical research sample, and still having time to work on your comics. It seems like you're not going to make it—but you will.

Go with your gut feeling about what is right for you when opportunities come up. Always be sure to be proud of the art you're creating.

If you take a job you don't believe in, you won't be able to take your dream television-writing job that you'll be offered a month later. And two years after that, you'll get a publishing contract and actually make money from your comics. Follow your heart, and you can't go wrong.

Definition happy,
Ariel

• * •

Plum Sykes

Author

"Loud, pushy adults are not as popular as popular, teen extroverts."

IF YOU are one of the thousands of women and girls who enjoyed *Bergdorf Blondes*, my guess is you didn't brag about it. A light soufflé of a novel about rich, self-absorbed, and highly groomed Manhattan Ms.'s dying to become Mrs.'s, it's not what you'd typically recommend to your book group.

Don't confuse the blithe entertainment with its creator, Plum Sykes, however. British-born, Oxford-educated, Plum couldn't sound less like spoiled "moi," the book's main character. As a *Vogue* fashion-writer and regular on the Manhattan social circuit, she clearly has had a ringside seat to New York's circus of excess. But it takes a deft touch to skewer the 10021 zip code with humor rather than venom. Example: "Before you know it, you're out every night, working like crazy and secretly waxing the hair on the inside of your nose like everyone else."

Bergdorf Blondes became even more likable once I learned that Plum wrote it, longhand, while recovering from a painful broken engagement and 9/11's aftermath. "Some of the lines in the book are not too far from reality," she said. "My fiancé really did say, 'I find my cat more interesting than you.'"

Born Victoria, she was nicknamed Plum because a variety of the fruit is called Victoria. She grew up in Kent with five siblings, one of whom is Lucy, an unidentical twin who also lives in Manhattan and launched a baby's and children's clothing line in 2004.

With wide-set brown eyes, a narrow, ballerina-like torso, and charmingly imperfect teeth, Plum reminds me of Jackie Onassis in the 1970s. On this February day, Plum's wearing a knit cap pulled down to her eyebrows and a long skinny scarf wound around her neck. Despite the predictably appealing British accent and intimidating social pedigree, she seems very easy to talk to.

Since *Bergdorf Blondes*, she has married and had her first child, a daughter named Ursula, who was only four months old when we met. She isn't at all saccharine about her new role, insisting briskly that she has no interest in writing about motherhood or children. In addition to books—her second, *Debutante Divorcée*, was published in 2006—she continues to write for American *Vogue* and was on her way to a story meeting after our get-together.

Now thirty-eight, Plum's letter is written to herself at seventeen when her shyness so imprisoned her that it felt like a physical affliction.

Dear Plum,

   It's beyond tragic to be the quiet one when all other teenage girls are Popular Extroverts. Popular Extroverts do not flush when asked simple questions like "How's school going?" Their cheeks do not turn the color of a pinot noir grape if they win the history prize. They can talk casually to other teen humans. They don't mind getting up on stage in front of teen human's parents and doing things like tap dancing or pretending to be Juliet in *Romeo and Juliet.*

The thing that you don't know that I do is that popular teen extroverts turn into loud, pushy adults. Loud pushy adults are not as popular as popular teen extroverts. The truth is that being shy and quiet in childhood is seen from the adult world as charming and old-fashioned. It's so rare that it's even faintly mysterious. There are so many loud, pushy children and louder, pushier mothers that it's a relief to come across a child who doesn't need to force their tap dancing and acting ability on unwitting strangers. Really interesting people tend to be the quiet ones. They don't need to show off or shout about themselves because their talent speaks for itself.

It's chic to be shy.

Love,

A much less shy,
Plum

· ✳ ·

ASHLEY WARLICK
Author

*"You have not lost your mother and what she
knows about you."*

$\mathcal{B}$ORN IN Utah and raised in Charlotte, North Carolina,
novelist Ashley Warlick is a Southern girl who writes without
the drawl and cornpone. Sure, she can nail a South Carolinian
expression if she wants to. But to me her Southern roots are
most evident in the way she lays her hands on the unnamable
tumult beneath the surface of things. Her respect for the emotional eddies and lawless calculus that so often govern behavior makes you feel she'd be a forgiving friend.

Here is one of her characters talking about the months after
her sister's murder, from Ashley's second novel, *The Summer
After June*:

*Since June died she seemed to be living through flood or famine,
a disaster brought on by too much or too little. She had tried being
angry about that, then sorry for herself, then just sorry. She tried all
her old tricks for grief, but they were only tricks. The grief in her
was smarter than that.*

Her first novel, *The Distance from the Heart of Things*—for
which she became the youngest ever recipient of the
Houghton Mifflin Literary Fellowship—was published in
1996 when she was twenty-three. *The Summer After June* came

out in 2000 and *Seek the Living* in 2005. In a departure, her next novel is loosely based on the life of M.F.K. Fisher, the food author and writer. She says it's new for her, but then again, this is someone who once took cookbook author Nigella Lawson's *How to Eat* to the gym and read it like a novel. I can't wait to see what food sounds like once it's been filleted by Ashley.

When we spoke, Ashley had recently returned from a vacation in Spain (the Manchego cheese, croquettes, octopus, and clara were her favorites), navigated through her four-year-old's strep throat, and dived into teaching her workshop at the South Carolina Governor's School for the Arts and Humanities, a public residential high school in Greenville where she lives. She also teaches in the MFA program at Queens University in Charlotte.

Now thirty-five, Ashley's letter is written to herself at seventeen, when she was a senior at a tony private school, during a time when her family had begun to experience a change in fortune.

Dear Ashley—

It's like this. You get up in the morning, and you put on your dad's flannel shirt, you skip breakfast and drive yourself to school. You put your stuff in the locker next to the locker of the guy who used to be your friend, and then your boyfriend in middle school, and who is now somebody who doesn't even really say hello.

His mother is dying, and you want to tell him how sorry you are because she was always nice to you when he was your friend, your boyfriend. Your mother was nice to him, too, even that time he talked you into making out (not talked really; no words were used in the convincing) in the back of your mother's van while she was driving you to a basketball game. You were embarrassed when she said *do you really think I don't know what's going on*, but honestly, the idea hadn't occurred to you until she said it, and then you burst into tears. Just like when you will finally catch the right moment to say *I'm sorry your mom is dying*. You'll start crying then, too, and what exactly you're crying for is hard to say.

For the rest of your life you will see relationships split open and fall away, like when drought pulls the ground away from a fencepost, like when a wound opens. It's a hard thing to understand, this kind of loss where people don't really go anywhere. Right now, you think you're not friends anymore because you're not skinny, and this is partly true. You're not skinny, because you're not made that way: It's just a fact. You will never be skinny—you will be flirtatious and smart and easy to be around, get married, have children, write novels, teach classes, cook, knit, vacation in foreign countries. But you will never be friends with this guy again. To think it has something to do with the size of your jeans or how you spend your Saturday nights is no better than thinking his mother brought her cancer on herself.

Notice how your mother asks about his mother often, as though he might have confided in you suddenly, there at your shared lockers. She knows you are no longer friends. She knows you think it's because you are no longer skinny. She knows, truly, what is going on, but she asks about his mother anyway, because it is a question more about herself, your family, what would happen if this were to happen to us, instead of what has.

For all the things you've lost in the last few years—
the country club membership, the big brick house, the
tiny cars, the security—you have not lost this. You have
not lost your mother and what she knows about you.
Some days, it is as if you've been to war together, and
maybe all families are like that, but the thing you will
learn is that all families don't come out the other side
holding on to each other. It is hard to hold on to one
another while slipping and teetering, your own balance
being so strong. The easier thing to do is fall away.

Ashley

· ✳ ·

KIMBERLY WILLIAMS-PAISLEY

Actress

*"Being treated as a dork
will color who you are forever."*

$\mathcal{F}$ROM an adult's perspective, mean-girl behavior all looks the same. But victims know better: Middle school and high school meanness is highly calibrated to its target. For Kimberly Williams-Paisley, star of *Father of the Bride, We Are Marshall*, and *How to Eat Fried Worms* movies and Dana on *According to Jim*, the suffering started just before seventh grade when she was about to enter Fieldston, a private school in Riverdale, New York, that she attended for two years.

She was one of a handful of new girls entering the class (another was Sofia Coppola). Kimberly's mother had met another mom, who invited Kimberly to a pool party in order to introduce her to the nice girls in class. "I was the only one who showed up with my mom," Kimberly remembers. The girls decided to have a diving contest. Kimberly had not taken diving lessons but nevertheless decided to go for it. She stepped out onto the diving board and executed one of the worst belly flops of her life. She recalls slapping the water, feeling the horrible burn, and dreading coming to the surface to face all those girls looking at her.

"They all had looks of disdain and horror. One of them asked with exaggerated concern, 'Are you all right?' But their expressions said that that was the ugliest thing they had ever seen," says Kimberly. The belly flop may as well have sealed her fate. She could never get it right after that. She adored the school's dance and theater program, as well as its buildings, which were filled with colorful nooks and crannies. But she could never fit in.

Growing up to become a movie star helps, though. Immensely. Married to country singer Brad Paisley, who wrote the tender *She's Everything* for her, Kimberly laughed when I asked her if she ever wondered whether those mean girls know what the girl they once rejected had become. Turns out she happened to run into one of the former Popular Girls. Kimberly was coming off the set of *Father of the Bride* on her way to a screening when it happened. "She was *so* nice to me," remembers Kimberly. "Of course, I played it cool and was very nice to her . . . but inside my little child was jumping for joy. It didn't hurt that a professional had done my hair and makeup that day."

Those days seem like a lifetime ago. Eight months pregnant when I talked to her, Kimberly and Brad are immersed in their family; William Huckleberry Paisley was born February 22, 2007.

Now thirty-six, Kimberly's letter is to the new girl she once was in middle school.

*

Dear Kim,

I see you in the nurse's office with your daily stomachache—the real one you often suffer from, or the fake one you develop to get out of things. You know that being at Fieldston is a privilege, one that your family can only afford for two years. But your body is shouting out how miserable you are here.

Gym is the worst. You can never make those horrible orange uniforms look cool, the way the popular girls do with bleaching and just the right roll of the sleeves. You're mortified about taking your clothes off. Everyone checks each other out. It hasn't happened yet, but soon the thought of gym is going to start making you break out in hives. So then you have to undress while covered in red bumps.

It seems that every small detail prevents you from fitting in. You've turned into the unpopular geek. In field hockey season, everyone showed up with cute little sticks. Your parents made you bring your mom's old, giant stick—the one that looks like an ice hockey stick. For softball you had to use her old, heavy, smelly mitt. You are left-handed, and the mitt is made for a right-handed player, and so what little athletic talent you have was further hindered.

You're not exactly paralyzed about what a big belly flop you are at this school. There is a sweet naïveté that protects you from knowing how *out* you are. But not fitting in is so unexplainable, so perplexing, and *so* much harder than you ever expected, that it's making you fearful of the future. If *this* part of life is so hard, you think to yourself, how much harder will your life get in the future?

This, my friend, is the big leagues. Twenty-five years later I know that what you're going through really is as hard as it gets. If you can get through this, you really can endure anything. There will definitely be difficult things you'll have to face, but going forward you'll be able to put them into perspective.

So when that boy you have a crush on looks at you, nudges his friend, and the friend rolls his eyes like *Puhleese, you can't be serious,* try to hang in there. Everything is going to change for you at your next school. You'll find your people. You'll fit in. In fact, you'll be homecoming queen. How unimaginable is that? And that's just the beginning for you.

Being treated as a dork will color who you are forever. You'll know that you are a survivor. You'll fear fewer things. You'll have a great dose of humility, and you'll understand vulnerability—which will be crucial to the creative person you will become.

You won't be able to appreciate this now, but you'll also have some hilarious stories that you and your family and your friends will howl over.

Dorks forever!

Love,
Kim

· ✳ ·

ELISABETH WITHERS

Singer/Actress

*"Girlhood can be wasted on people and things
not worth your prime time in life."*

$\mathcal{A}$T FIVE, she began belting out songs along with Aretha
Franklin, Barbra Streisand, and other vocalists from her parents' record collection. Elisabeth Withers was hell-bent on a
singing career, even though her family was oriented toward
math and science. She was a middle child, between two brothers and a sister. Her mother—The Glue of the Family, as Elisabeth calls her—is a mathematical engineer. Her sister went
into chemistry, one brother became a mathematician, and the
other became a doctor.

By the time she was in high school, Elisabeth was busy creating her own world as fast as she could. The walls and ceiling
of her all-pink room in the family's Joliet, Illinois, ranch style
house, were plastered with cut-out photographs of shoes, belts,
purses, and other fashions from *Vogue* and *GQ,* as well as
images of her favorite actors and musicians. She had a beautiful, wooden bed that sat high off the floor, a pink sham, and a
mirror that figured importantly in her fantasy life. "It was so
huge that I would do all my pretend magazine interviews
while looking into it. I would interview myself about being a
singer," recalls Elisabeth.

In the mornings the family would sit down together for oatmeal, sausage, eggs, toast, and homemade jelly prepared by her mother from apple and pear trees in the back yard. Then Elisabeth's father, a political broker, would escort her to the 7:05 a.m. train headed into Chicago, where he would take her to her high school before going into his office. At the end of the day, they traveled home together sometimes making up songs about their days. "At seventeen, I was very focused—never one to follow a defined path. I was never one of the girls to wear what everyone else was wearing, or do what everyone else was doing because it was cool. I just loved being me, playing make-believe, and dreaming of leaving my small town of Joliet to sing. I wanted to trail-blaze," she says.

In 1993 her focus and talent won her a scholarship to the Berklee College of Music, in Boston, after which she raced through a master's program at New York University. "I felt I was ready to live my dream. I wanted to sing rock, R&B, hip-hop, the blues, gospel—it didn't matter. I wanted to sing," she recalls.

Unlike so many other aspiring vocalists, Elisabeth developed a solid book of business right away, which quickly bloomed into much more. She began writing and singing the demo vocals for Cher—which led to singing backup for Celine Dion, Jennifer Lopez, and Mary J. Blige, among others. Soon after she began opening up for well-known artists and musicians, she was invited to audition for the role of Shug Avery in Oprah Winfrey's Broadway musical *The Color Purple*. "I had never acted a day in my life," Elisabeth says, with a giggle. "I didn't know who I was competing against, but I just knew I wanted the challenge of that role."

Three auditions later, Elisabeth got the role, later earning a Tony Award nomination for her performance. The frosting on the cake: a recording contract with Blue Note Records in 2004. The CEO of the company signed Elisabeth sight-unseen. Reflecting this magical, anything-is-possible ascent, she decided to title her most recent CD *It Can Happen To Anyone.*

Elisabeth, now in her thirties and a mother, writes to herself between the ages of sixteen and seventeen, during the transition from girl to woman.

Dear Liz,

The world is gonna keep spinning on its axis but sometimes to enjoy it all, you have to slow down and smell the roses. Listen. Everything you need is right there in your heart, speaking to you and answering every question. You are a child of God, so trust that. Enjoy the moment. Every moment you are placed in—enjoy it. Because that moment is preparing you for the next moment.

For fun, learn how to play cards or chess. Read the *New York Times* (as Daddy would say). Learn how to swim. Learn French or Spanish.

Laugh and take time to really get to know your friends. I know life can get really busy sometimes, but pop a card in the mail to them. Send an email or a text. Maybe squeeze in a coffee date just to catch up on things and say hello. Remember your friend Amanda from the Chicago Academy for the Arts? Now she was a real friend. You so enjoyed her. She was brilliant. But she was a senior when you were a sophomore. She graduated and was gone in the blink of an eye. Don't let that happen with your other friends.

And Liz, here's one you won't like: Don't grow up too fast. It's fine to have ambition and drive, but hold on to your girlhood as long as you can. 'Cause "womanhood" is a lifetime. Girlhood can be wasted on people and things not worth your prime time in life. You can date and see people, but I wouldn't have sex at your age. Getting that close to a guy monopolizes your time, your energy, and your emotions.

Those precious resources should be spent enriching and exploring your world in more depth. OK, I won't preach to you but I will say that you've got all the tools to enjoy this beautiful thing called life!

Love,
Elisabeth

· ✳ ·

A Letter To *Your* Younger Self . . .
What would you say? Send your letter to
info@letterstomyyoungerself.com